1976

THE COMMONWEALTH AND INTERNATIONAL LIBRARY
Joint Chairmen of the Honorary Editorial Advisory Board
SIR ROBERT ROBINSON, O.M., F.R.S., LONDON
DEAN ATHELSTAN SPILHAUS, MINNESOTA
Publisher: ROBERT MAXWELL, M.C., M.P.

PERGAMON OXFORD GERMAN SERIES
General Editors: C. V. RUSSELL, W. D. HALLS

THE PLAYS OF GRILLPARZER

THE PLAYS
OF GRILLPARZER

by

GEORGE A. WELLS

Professor of German at the University of London

1966
THE QUEEN'S AWARD
TO INDUSTRY 1966

PERGAMON PRESS

LONDON · OXFORD · EDINBURGH · NEW YORK
TORONTO · SYDNEY · PARIS · BRAUNSCHWEIG

Pergamon Press Ltd., Headington Hill Hall, Oxford
4 & 5 Fitzroy Square, London W.1

Pergamon Press (Scotland) Ltd., 2 & 3 Teviot Place, Edinburgh 1

Pergamon Press Inc., Maxwell House, Fairview Park, Elmsford,
New York 10523

Pergamon of Canada Ltd., 207 Queen's Quay West, Toronto 1

Pergamon Press (Aust.) Pty. Ltd., 19a Boundary Street,
Rushcutters Bay, N.S.W. 2011, Australia

Pergamon Press S.A.R.L., 24 rue des Écoles, Paris 5^e

Vieweg & Sohn GmbH, Burgplatz 1, Braunschweig

Printed in Great Britain by A. Wheaton & Co., Exeter

CONTENTS

MOTTO

Mir ist auf der Welt nichts zuwiderer als die weithergeholten Deutungen dichterischer Werke. Ein guter Dichter ist im Stande zu sagen was er will, und was er mit Absicht verbirgt, soll man nicht gewaltsam hervorziehen, am wenigsten aber als Hauptsache in den Vordergrund stellen. Die Poesie ist eben die Gestaltung des Gedankens, der Gedanke aber geht zwar immer über die Gestalt hinaus, aber das nächstliegende, natürlichste ist immer das wahrste.

(Grillparzer, II, 11, 112–13, *Tgb.*)

FOREWORD

Franz Grillparzer (1791–1872), although the most famous Austrian dramatist, has attracted relatively little attention in Britain, and there is not, to my knowledge, an English monograph on the effectiveness of his plays. Douglas Yates' book correlates the plays with their author's personal experiences, and is not primarily concerned with dramatic technique. In the present volume I have tried to fill this gap. In the first three chapters I discuss the three main types of play Grillparzer wrote, and in Chapter 5 I attempt some generalizations about what characterizes his tragedies and makes them effective. In the intervening Chapter 4 I discuss the salient features of his dramatic technique by reference to a single play, and I have selected *Die Jüdin von Toledo* for this purpose because it does in fact illustrate his methods so well. *Libussa*, which is, in contrast, quite atypical, is the subject of the brief final section of this chapter.

Although what I have written is very straightforward, much of it is not generally agreed. For instance, *Die Ahnfrau* is widely regarded as a fate-tragedy, the cause of Sappho's suicide has been frequently misunderstood, the character of Rudolf II has been repeatedly regarded as inconsistent, the relation between Grillparzer's theory and practice in tragedy has not been properly appreciated, nor have the principles which guided his treatment of history in his historical dramas. It is premature to write about specialized niceties until agreement has been reached on these fundamentals, and I hope this book will provoke discussion which may lead to such agreement.

Grillparzer is quoted from the standard edition of A. Sauer, *Grillparzers Werke*, im Auftrage der Reichshaupt- und Residenzstadt (Wien, 1905, etc.). The reference I, 7, 188 would be to division I, volume 7, page 188 of this edition. The references to lines of Grillparzer's plays are given according to the numbering in this edition. Some other editors count the broken lines differently, so that their whole numbering is different.

For bibliographies of the secondary literature I refer the reader to the *Jahrbuch der Grillparzer-Gesellschaft* (Wien, 1937), XXXIV and (Wien, 1953), I (Folge III). The former covers the years 1905–37 and the latter 1937–52. More recent literature is given by Joachim Müller, *Grillparzer* (Stuttgart, 1963), and in Herbert Seidler's "Forschungsbericht", *Zeitschrift für deutsche Philologie*, LXXXIII (1964). Some of the most recent literature is listed in the short bibliography in Eleonore Frey-Staiger's *Grillparzer: Gestalt und Gestaltung des Traums* (Zürich, 1966), and the longer one in Ulrich Fülleborn's *Das Dramatische Geschehen im Werke Grillparzers* (München, 1966).

Some of the material included in Chapter 3 appeared in *German Life and Letters*, XI (1958) and a small amount of Chapter 1 has been published in the *Journal of English and Germanic Philology*, LXIV (1965). I am indebted to the editors of both journals for permission to reprint. I am also glad to record my thanks to Irene Wells, and to my colleagues Miss Margaret Jacobs, Professor R. Tymms, Professor W. D. Robson-Scott, Dr. G. P. Butler, Mr. A. Stillmark and Mr. B. Thompson for their criticism of parts of my manuscript.

CHAPTER 1

THE PLAYS OF ACTION

1. The Plays for the Popular Stage

Grillparzer published two plays for the popular stage, *Die Ahnfrau* and *Der Traum ein Leben*. The former was written within three weeks in 1816 and first performed in 1817 at the Theater an der Wien—one of the surburban theatres of Vienna—not at the Burgtheater, which was reserved for more serious drama and according to an edict of Joseph II in 1776 was to "further good taste and moral ennoblement". *Der Traum ein Leben,* begun in 1817 and completed in 1831, was first performed at the Burgtheater, but not until 1834, since the management was long unwilling to accept such a play for this theatre.

The Viennese popular stage usually provided fairies and magic (Mozart's *Magic Flute* is a good example) and also clowning and improvization. These features were even introduced into serious drama, and in 1763 Lessing's tragedy *Miss Sara Sampson* was played with Hanswurst replacing the part of Norton! (See ref. 40, pp. 153, 383.) Grillparzer's plays for this stage have some magic and supernatural elements, but no clowning, for he could not abide anything banal. For this reason these, like all his plays, are in verse—four-foot trochees in these two plays and five-foot iambs (for the most part) in his others. Furthermore, if I may use the word "action" in the sense of "outer action"—actions which advance the plot, not 'inner action' or psychological processes in the characters—then the two popular plays may be said to be characterized by their exciting action; the emphasis is on what the characters do, rather than on the people they are. In general, a distinction can be made between plays with exciting action but

1

where the characters are uninteresting, and those where the characters are drawn in detail but fail to do anything of interest. The ideal lies, perhaps, between the two extremes, and is achieved by Grillparzer in his historical dramas. In his plays for the popular stage he neglects character—at any rate to some extent—in favour of action, while in his Greek plays the reverse is the case.

Die Ahnfrau is the first play he published, but he had already completed *Blanka von Kastilien*, a tragedy written, as he himself confessed, in imitation of Schiller's *Don Carlos*. The situation and behaviour of the hero, Fedriko, is similar to that of Schiller's Carlos. Both feel a conflict between their passion and their loyalty to their king, both seek the king's confidence and are offended by his unwillingness to trust them; and both are led to take part in an already existing rebellion caused by the harshness of his rule. The style of Grillparzer's play owes as much to Schiller as does its content. It is well illustrated by the monologue in Act I, scene 2, where Fedriko, having treated a courtier with disdain, explains that he has sacrificed everything to virtue:

> Kein holdes Weib steht liebend mir zur Seite
> Und hilft des Lebens Stürme mir bekämpfen,
> Und streichelt mir des düstern Unmuths Falten
> Mit süßem Lächeln von der finstern Stirne.

The immaturity of the writer is clear from the way he tickets each of the principal nouns with a conventional epithet: "holdes Weib", süßes Lächeln", and so on. The speaker then adds another illustration of his sacrifices:

> Kein muntrer Knabe jauchzet mir entgegen,
> Den theuren Vater kindisch froh umhüpfend.

Here again are the conventional epithets; and as one would expect a man who renounces marriage in order to do his duty to be without children, this illustration does not so much convey new information as drive the point home in an attempt to rouse the sympathy of the audience. This long-windedness is characteristic of many dramas of this period which reproduced the heroism, idealism, rhetoric and loquaciousness of the heroes of Schiller's historical dramas. In E. T. A. Hoffmann's *Nachricht von den neusten Schicksalen des Hundes Berganza,* the dog complains of the mediocrity of these imitations, and the author replies that their long-windedness is a sort of pregnancy, in that each line of verse seems to give birth to ten more. A good example occurs in Fedriko's peroration, where the final couplet that makes the whole intelligible is repeatedly postponed by clauses introduced with "was":

> Denn was das süßeste dem Menschen ist,
> Was ihm die Leiden minder lastend macht,
> Was jede Freude tausendfach erhöht,
> Den Trieben der Natur, der Menschlichkeit
> Hab' ich entsagt.

The language of the play shows other traces of Schiller's influence. It is full of sharp antitheses ("Himmel und Hölle", "Licht und Dunkel", "Engel und Teufel") and the genitive frequently precedes the noun it qualifies ("des Lebens Stürme", "des Unmuthes Falten"), making the speech (at least to the present-day reader) sound much more elevated than normal discourse. Personification is also frequent, and this is very characteristic of the dramatists who imitated Schiller at this time. Stahl, whose *Das Schauspiel der Schillerepigonen* sums up this chapter of German theatrical history, remarks that "wo einem Afterdichter die Fähigkeit abging, einen klaren Vergleich aufzustellen, da war er immer noch imstande, irgendein Abstraktum auf eine stupide Weise zu konkretisieren".*

Grillparzer began to turn away from Schiller in 1810, after completing *Blanka.* A diary entry for 19 June criticizes *Kabale und Liebe* as "das elendeste Machwerk das je ein Mann . . . aus bunten, glitzenden Lumpen zusammengeflikt hat, und an dessen breiten Worten und hohen Stelzen man unmöglich die Absicht des Verfassers, ein Meisterwerk liefern zu wollen, erkennen kann" (II, 7, 48). It is not merely that a play in prose where the heroine is poisoned by a glass of lemonade was bound to appear banal to Grillparzer, who continued to abhor the *bürgerliches Trauerspiel,* as a genre, for the rest of his life. The passage shows that he found the rhetoric and declamation equally distasteful. And he went on

*Ref. 44, p. 209; cf. refs. 25 and 35, pp. 24–5.

to complain of the "bombastischer Wortschwall in der *Braut von Messina*". Nevertheless, he obviously had not grown to full independence by the time he wrote *Die Ahnfrau*, which retains a number of the weaknesses of *Blanka*—for instance, the tedious length of some of the speeches. Old Borotin takes nineteen lines to tell us that he will not survive the winter:

> Wohl wird sich das Jahr erneuen   (l. 42)
>
> .   .   .   .
>
> Nie erneut sich Borotin,   (l. 60),

and when Jaromir admits that he is a robber, he goes on saying so for over a hundred lines. Moreover, the imagery is full of the personified abstractions that abound in the plays of Schiller's imitators. Fear, "mit Vampir-Rüssel", sucks the blood from Jaromir's veins (ll. 757–8). The "schlaferwachtes Auge" of Bertha's "Neigung" has lighted upon him (ll. 1146–7), and there is mention of "der Rachsucht gift'ger Hauch", "des Hasses Atem" (ll. 1293–4), and "der Sorge Natterzahn" (l. 1507). In Jaromir's long monologue in Act V, "Laster", "Hinterlist", "Neid", "Mord", "Meineid", and "Gotteslästrung" are all personified in a catalogue reminiscent of the baroque lyric of the seventeenth century.

To understand *Die Ahnfrau* it will be necessary to discuss its relation to fate-tragedy. The origin of the idea of fate can be readily surmised. The consciousness of a certain power in oneself of choosing between one act and another, represented as the "will", suggested a similar power presiding over the world at large. In *Oedipus Rex* the outcome is determined by a power of this kind, a power which is malignant in the extreme. Elsewhere[53] I have tried to show that the same is true of Schiller's *Die Braut von Messina* (1803), inspired as it was by Sophocles' play. And Schiller's play in turn acted as a source of inspiration to the fate-tragedies that dominated the German stage for fifteen years or more after his death.

In these plays, someone pronounces a curse on a whole family whereupon a malignant supernatural power ensures that it is effective by sending catastrophes which tend to occur on the same day of the year and are often brought about by one and the same fatal weapon. Zacharias Werner's *Der* 24. *Februar*, written in 1809, is often taken as typical. Here we learn that a son was sharpening his scythe with a knife when his father provoked him. He threw the knife and the father died (at midnight on 24 February) cursing his son, the son's wife and their progeny. A son (with the mark of a blood-red scythe on his arm) is duly born to the young couple, and the action on the stage culminates in his murder by his father, at midnight on 24 February, with the same fatal knife. We may ask, with Carlyle,[7, p. 346] why the family had not "during all that half century . . . carried it to the smithy to make hobnails; but kept it hanging on a peg, most injudiciously . . . almost as a sort of bait and bonus to Satan, a ready-made fulchrum for whatever machinery he might bring to bear against them". But the text has anticipated the question and informed us that the family has become so impoverished that only this knife remains to them (l. 297)! The misfortunes leading over the years to this impoverishment all occurred on 24 February (ll. 555-6).

Werner's play comprises a single Act: the unities of time and place are kept. In fact the action lasts only one hour, from eleven until twelve midnight. It was Lessing who said that a play which keeps the conventions of French classical tragedy (in particular the unities) need not necessarily be effective. There could be no better illustration of the justice of this statement than *Der 24. Februar*.

Müllner's *Der 29. Februar* (1812) makes the catastrophes even less likely to be mere coincidences by placing them on a day which is only available once every four years. It tells how (in Carlyle's words) "some old Woodcutter or Forester has fallen into deadly sin with his wife's sister, long ago, on that intercalary day," for which reason "his whole progeny must, wittingly or unwittingly, proceed in incest and murder; the day of the catastrophe regularly occurring every four years on the same twenty-ninth; till happily the whole are murdered and there is an end".[7, pp. 347-8] There is a novel element, as compared with *Der 24. Februar.* The family does not only lie under a curse, but the exact details of the three worst catastrophes are foretold by dreams. The effect of this is clearly to reinforce the impression of fatal inevitability. If the mother dreams of the death of her daughter occurring in the precise circumstances in which the girl is later to die, then it looks as though the dream is giving her insight into an event which has been decreed by fate, the more so as the parents were not present when the girl fell to her death (11. 550–5), and so could not have caused her to do so because of any nervousness on their part, due to their consciousness of the prophetic dream.

In plays such as this where an evil end is not only fated to occur but predicted in detail, the interest will be at least as much in the plot as in the characters. As in *Oedipus Rex* interest will be directed towards the manner in which the unlikely seeming prophecies of doom will be fulfilled. Neither in Werner's nor in Müllner's play is there much attempt to draw character. Thus the wife is, as Minor put it,[28, p. iv] little more than a type—"das schwache von jedem Windzuge und jeder Ahnung geängstigte Weib". Both plays begin with an expression of her terror at the failure of husband or son to come home. These fears prove vain, for the missing member of the family soon returns, but not before the atmosphere of terror has been set. So we see that in both cases the wife is not so much a character of interest as a means of creating the necessary atmosphere. Minor says (and the statement is certainly true of Müllner's play) that in both the stranger who turns out to be a long-lost relative is equally colourless, a mere "Notbehelf" of the plot, with about as much character of his own as a confidant in French classical tragedy.

Apart from lacking memorable characters, Werner and Müllner's fate-tragedies are ineffective because they labour the fate-principle to the exclusion of all else, and also, as Carlyle saw, because they place it in a bourgeois setting. He noted that "the Fate of the Greeks, though a false, was a lofty hypothesis" and that:

> with them the avenging Power dwelt, at least in its visible manifestations, among the high places of the earth; visiting only kingly houses and world

criminals, from whom it might be supposed the world, but for such miraculous interferences, could have exacted no vengeance. . . . Never, that we recollect of, did the Erinnyes become mere sheriff's officers, and Fate a justice of the peace, haling poor drudges to the treadmill for robbery of hen-roosts, or scattering the earth with steel-traps to keep down poaching.

His final verdict on Müllner is worth recording:

The value of Müllner's Fate-tenet as a dramatic principle may be estimated . . . by this one consideration: that in these days no person . . . believes it. . . . We are not contending that fiction should become fact, or that no dramatic incident is genuine unless it could be sworn to before a jury; but simply that fiction should not be falsehood and delirium. How shall any one, in the drama or in poetry of any sort, present a consistent philosophy of life, which is the soul and ultimate essence of all poetry, if he and every mortal know that the whole moral basis of his ideal world is a lie? And is it other than a lie that man's life is, was or could be, grounded on this pettifogging principle of a Fate that pursues woodcutters and cowherds with miraculous visitations on stated days of the month? Can we, with any profit, hold the mirror up to Nature in this wise? When our mirror is no mirror, but only as it were a nursery saucepan, and that long since grown rusty? [7, pp. 349–50]

Grillparzer's play certainly has obvious affinities with the German fate-tragedies. First, the verse is that of Müllner's play, and Grillparzer confessed that he would not have dared to use these Spanish trochees for the German stage without Müllner's example (I, 16, 120). Furthermore, the action is centred on one family and includes incest and parricide, and there is a stranger who turns out to be a long-lost relative—all familiar motifs of the fate-tragedy. The eerie atmosphere of fate-tragedy is set in the opening stage directions, which specify a "gothische Halle" —the Gothic being associated with darkness and fear—on a snowy winter night and which also tell that "an einer Kulisse des Vordergrundes hängt ein verrosteter Dolch in seiner Scheide". This is the fatal weapon with which the ancestress was killed long ago, carefully preserved to be the instrument of another catastrophe during the play. In the opening scene old Count Borotin talks about the death and misfortune he feels helpless to avert from himself and his family. He is sure that fate has determined to extinguish them all. The gloom of this setting is reinforced by the horrific imagery. The earth in its blanket of snow is likened to a corpse in a shroud, and the starless sky to hollow empty eyes which look blackly down on the huge grave, the earth.

Grillparzer also does his best to keep our nerves on edge by the way he develops the action. Just when the family servant is telling of the ancestress' habit of walking as a ghost and knocking at night, a hullabaloo is heard outside. The juxtaposition is clearly intended to make us jump out of our skins, although it transpires that the noise was made by Jaromir.

Carlyle's resumé gives the essentials of the plot:

> Count Borotin is really a worthy prosing old gentleman; only he had a son long ago drowned in a fishpond (body not found); and has still a highly accomplished daughter, whom there is none offering to wed, except one Jaromir, a person of unknown extraction, and to all appearances of the lightest purse; nay, as it turns out afterwards, actually the head of a Banditti establishment, which had long infested the neighbouring forests. However, a Captain of foot arrives at this juncture, utterly to root out these Robbers; and now the strangest things come to light. For who should this Jaromir prove to be but poor old Borotin's drowned son; not drowned, but stolen and bred up by these Outlaws; the brother, therefore, of his intended; a most truculent fellow, who fighting for his life unwittingly kills his own father, and drives his bride to poison herself: In which wise . . . he cannot get married. The reader sees, all this is not to be accomplished without some jarring and tumult. In fact there is a frightful uproar everwhere throughout that night; robbers dying, musketry discharging, women shrieking, men swearing, and the Ahnfrau herself emerging at intervals as the genius of the whole discord. But time and hours bring relief, as they always do. Jaromir, in the long-run, likewise succeeds in dying: whereupon the whole Borotin lineage having gone to the Devil, the Ancestress also retires thither.(7, pp. 328–9)

Act IV brings one disclosure after another: first we learn that old Borotin has been wounded, then that he knows that it was Jaromir who wounded him; and finally he is told that Jaromir is his son. Grillparzer has clearly taken *Die Braut von Messina* as his model for this succession of tragic revelations.* The dying count declares that Jaromir's deed, and, presumably, all the apparent coincidences on which it was based, were engineered by fate, and that the lad is therefore not to blame (ll. 2541–3).

*For this and other observations on *Die Ahnfrau* I am indebted to Kohm.(23)

Another feature that *Die Ahnfrau* shares with the conventional fate-tragedy is that the emphasis is on the plot and action, which is continually advanced by the arrival of new characters—Jaromir, the captain, Walther, the soldier with the piece of scarf, and finally Boleslav, who is introduced repeatedly in order to further the action. Thus he is captured so as to reveal to the old count that Jaromir is a Borotin; he escapes in order to make the same disclosure to Jaromir himself; and he is then recaptured in order to put the soldiers on Jaromir's track! The action develops so swiftly that the unity of time is kept, and the first change of scene comes only in Act V. In this play Grillparzer certainly keeps his later formulated principle of not splitting the action into a number of disconnected episodes which have to be linked by the imagination of the reader or audience (see below, p. 145).

Occasionally the action is held up while the characters struggle against accepting some truth that has just been revealed to them. The dying count tries not to believe that it is his son who has knifed him; in a long monologue in Act V Jaromir resists the realization that he has killed his own father, and tries to suppress the truth by thinking of his love for Bertha, asking how she could possibly be his sister, as he desires her so passionately. But in spite of such details of psychological interest, the emphasis is on the action, and the characters are not drawn in great detail, most of them embodying a single fundamental trait or mood. The captain is seriously and straightforwardly devoted to his duty, Bertha full of vigour and anxious to enjoy her young life. The old count tells that she is also patient, long-suffering and understanding (ll. 411–16)—a trait which has the function of motivating her acceptance of Jaromir's excuses for being a robber. Jaromir's chief characteristic is his lack of restraint and self-control, repeatedly expressed in his behaviour (e.g. ll. 800–12, 1323 ff.). The count is the most complex character. He is, first and foremost, melancholy and full of foreboding, and is made to appear in this light to set the atmosphere of doom. But his other traits include straightforward honesty (ll. 280–1), strong loyalty (ll. 1170, 1187, etc.), pride in his illustrious ancestors (ll. 1469 ff.), coupled with dejection at the decline of the family's fortunes. It is this pride that leads him to go out and fight the robbers, stung by the slur he thinks the captain has put upon his family honour (ll. 1494–8, 2304) and hence to be killed by his own son.

However, although Grillparzer's play has the atmosphere and accoutrements of a fate-tragedy, there is no decisive evidence that its tragic outcome is contrived by a malignant power. In the conventional fate-tragedies, as in *Die Braut von Messina*, someone puts a curse upon a particular family and fate makes it duly effective. In *Die Ahnfrau* there is no curse; there is a legend (l. 108) that the ancestress must atone for her adultery by walking as a ghost until all her descendants are dead. Grillparzer invites us to assume (without actually stating it) that fate has put this heavy sentence upon her. As Carlyle says, in his humorous way:

> This Ancestress is a lady, or rather the ghost of a lady, for she has been defunct some centuries, who in life had committed what we call an "indiscretion"; which indiscretion the unpolite husband punished, one would have thought sufficiently, by running her through the body. However, the *Schicksal* of Grillparzer does not think it sufficient, but further dooms the fair penitent to walk as goblin, till the last branch of her family be extinct. Accordingly, she is heard, from time to time, slamming doors and the like, and now and then, seen with dreadful goggle-eyes and other ghost-appurtenances, to the terror not only of the servant people, but of old Count Borotin, her now sole male descendant, whose afternoon nap she, on one occasion, cruelly disturbs.[7, p. 328]

The play also tells that she appears to her descendants to give warning of misfortune, which she can foresee but not avert (ll. 505–12). This leaves it open whether those she warns can avert it, or whether the whole outcome has been fated to occur. Old Borotin, we saw, believes the latter to be the case, and feels gloomy and helpless. But he may be wrong, and there is certainly no proof that fate is trying to ruin his whole family.

A little later (ll. 550 ff.) the old family servant tells that the descendants of the ancestress are the fruit of her adultery, not the legitimate offspring of her husband, and that this explains her punishment. The servant's idea is that she pretended that the son she bore was her husband's, so that the boy succeeded to the title. His last descendants (the characters in the play) are no more entitled to the estate than he, and the misfortunes they suffer are to that extent a just punishment for usurpation. This detail is absent from the original version, and Grillparzer inserted it because Schreyvogel had complained that there was no connection between the guilt of the ancestress and the sufferings of the last Borotins. She was simply condemned to appear as a ghost until they became extinct. It did not follow that they would kill each other; but since they do in fact die in this way, Schreyvogel suggested that their extinction be made into something of a divine chastisement, punishing the sins of the ancestress in a later generation. However, Grillparzer stresses in his autobiography that the servant's story is not necessarily true, so that, even in the revised version, there is no decisive evidence that fate is bent on contriving the family's doom. He says:

> Genau genommen nun, findet sich die Schicksalsidee gar nicht in der *Ahnfrau*. Wenn der Richterspruch gegen dieses geistige Wesen lautete, daß sie zu wandeln habe, bis ihr Haus *durch Verbrechen* ausstürbe, so hätten diese Verbrechen allerdings eine Notwendigkeit; da aber das Ende ihrer Strafe nur bis zum Aussterben ihres Hauses, gleichviel wann und wie, bestimmt ist, so ist der Zeitpunkt, und daß es durch Verbrechen geschieht, zufällig. Daß die Personen zufolge einer dunkeln Sage eines frühen Verschuldens sich einem Verhängnis verfallen glauben, bildet so wenig ein faktisches Schicksal, als Einer darum unschuldig ist, weil er sich für unschuldig ausgibt.*

He thus leaves it for us to decide whether or not the catastrophe is the work of fate, and it is clear that he did so deliberately; for he noted in 1817 that, while the ancients really believed in fate, we moderns have only a vague feeling ("dunkle Ahnung") that it might exist. But, he continued, if the characters in a play attribute their troubles (with some show of plausibility) to fate, then all the experiences and reflections underlying our half-belief in it

---

*I, 16, 125. In spite of this disclaimer, Yates holds that, even in the first version of *Die Ahnfrau*, the characters are "dominated by a fore-ordained fate against which they vainly struggle."[55, p. 29] His evidence for this view is that the count and Jaromir believe it to be so, and that the play has some of the machinery (e.g. the fatal weapon) of Werner and Müllner's fate-trage-dies. But Minor long ago pointed out that, in spite of such affinities, Grillparzer does not in fact commit himself to a supernatural malignant fate in this play.[27, pp. 59, 75] The views of other critics are summarized by Morris.[29, pp. 284 ff.]

are activated, and the idea begins to appear plausible. But since it is erroneous and cannot survive cold, rational scrutiny, the dramatist must avoid committing himself to it openly, and must never clearly and unambiguously make the action depend on it. Whatever the characters may believe, the spectator must always be able to choose between fate and natural antecedents as the causes of the events depicted.* The argument is similar to the one advanced by Lessing in Stück XI of the *Hamburgische Dramaturgie*, where he is trying to justify ghosts in modern plays. He concedes that, if we do not believe in ghosts, we cannot be moved by plays in which they appear. But, he adds, "der Same, sie zu glauben, liegt in uns allen". The man in the street may deride them by day, but will tremble when he hears ghost stories at night. The artist must make our "seed of belief" germinate, as Shakespeare does in *Hamlet*, where the ghost appears at the midnight hour and with all the concomitants we were taught as children to associate with ghosts. On the other hand, the ghost in Voltaire's *Semiramis* fails to breach our adult scepticism, for it is introduced in broad daylight, and also at a public meeting. Any old woman, says Lessing, could have told Voltaire that ghosts shun daylight and avoid public assemblies; and an entity which so offends against what we feel to be the habits of ghosts cannot appear credible to us.

The effectiveness of *Die Ahnfrau* thus depends on its evocation of what Grillparzer called "eigentlich absurde, aber durch ihr immerwährendes Vorkommen als in der innersten Natur des Menschen begründet anzusehende Vorstellungen". As examples of such ideas he lists not only fate but also "Strafe der Unthat bis ins späteste Geschlecht", "eine von den natürlichen Folgen der That verschiedene Nemesis" and "Gespensterglauben" (II, 10, 187). All these are suggested in the play. Another factor on which its effectiveness depends is irony. The fate-tragedy motif that the stranger is in fact the long-lost son enables the author to include passages which acquire special meaning to an audience which may be presumed to know the facts of which the

*II, 7, 122 (*Tgb.* 1817); I, 14, 15–19 (*Über das Fatum*, 1817).

characters long remain ignorant. And, as we saw, the swift and exciting action also makes for effectiveness—although sometimes the necessity of developing the action means that the characters do what the plot requires of them without plausible motives. In real life a man's actions are determined by his 'character' reacting with external circumstances, and we can seldom claim to know anyone's character sufficiently well to predict his behaviour with confidence. Hence the dramatist has considerable freedom of invention. Of the characters he presents to us we know only what he makes them say and do. We are faced with the task of deciding whether all the words and actions of any particular character in the play are consistent with any conceivable character. We can seldom say that the most improbable reactions are quite impossible. This allows writers to construct the most fantastic plays in which no serious attempt is made to portray consistent characters. My argument is that *Die Ahnfrau* goes some way in this direction; some of the deeds essential to the action are not really made plausible by the character-drawing.

An example of such artificiality of motivation is Bertha's behaviour to Jaromir in Act II. She complains of his silence and coldness—as if it were not perfectly intelligible that a man who has just twice seen a ghost should be shocked and not in the mood for tender demonstrations of affection. Fearing that he may be as fickle as a butterfly which rapidly turns from one flower to another, she wraps a scarf round him to "bind his wings", as she puts it. Now this gesture (ill-motivated as it is by fears which in the circumstances are unjustified) is essential to the plot. For Jaromir next learns that Walther, who will certainly recognize him as the robber-captain, is searching the castle; so he decides he must flee, and steals out, unarmed, into the night, where he is shot in the arm and has a fragment of the scarf torn from him. Wounded, he has to return to the castle and is revealed to Bertha as the robber he is when the piece of scarf is brought in by a soldier who was once a prisoner of the robbers, and had recognized the man wearing the scarf as their captain.

It is also striking that the robbers did not kill this soldier when he was their captive, even though they have killed so many and even wanted to kill little Jaromir when they captured him at the age of 3, so that he could not betray them to the authorities (ll. 2468–74). Their restraint towards their soldier-captive is thus implausible, but essential to the plot, for this man's survival enables Bertha to learn that Jaromir is a robber. Again, the timely revelation that Jaromir is the count's son would have prevented tragedy, but is excluded because Boleslav is captured too late. In a tragedy of this kind we can scarcely feel that the final catastrophe is inevitable—unless we suppose it determined not by natural antecedents, but by a malignant fate.

Artificiality of motivation is already apparent in the exposition of *Die Ahnfrau*. Graf Borotin spends forty lines telling Bertha his life history, although he himself points out that he has often told it to her before (ll. 150–2). She tells him her experiences at equal length and with like assurance that he already knows them all (l. 219). In Grillparzer's *Medea* there is also much recounting the past, but it is better motivated. Jason cries out for the happiness that was once his in his youth at Corinth, and at such times he naturally tells how it contrasts with his present wretchedness. Or Medea and Jason mention past details (e.g. the death of Pelias) in the course of an argument in which each blames the other for their present lot, and they both appeal to past facts to establish their own innocence. In this way the past is narrated only in the interest of the present situation, whereas in *Die Ahnfrau* the narration is not adapted to the needs of the present, but is—as Hebbel saw[17, p. 269]—forced and strained, a mere device to tell the audience what it needs to know.

In 1817 Grillparzer was strongly critical of such artificiality, and his criticism reads almost like an indictment of *Die Ahnfrau*. He wrote in his diary:

> Zum dramatischen Dialog ist . . . nicht genug, daß verschiedene Personen abwechselnd sprechen, sondern das was sie sagen muß unmittelbar aus ihrer gegenwärtigen Lage, aus ihrer gegenwärtigen Leidenschaft hervorgehen. (II, 7, 106.)

His later plays rarely offend against this precept.

Since I shall frequently have cause to discuss motivation, it will be as well to say at the outset that this question as to what motivates behaviour is a reasonable one to ask of any character created by Grillparzer. Admittedly, in real life actions occur without our being able to understand their necessity. But as Grillparzer noted in 1820, in an essay entitled *Das Wesen des Drama*, when we do not understand the causes of some real-life event, we nevertheless feel confident that it has adequate causes, if only we could discover them; whereas we know that the events of a play have been contrived by an author, and if we cannot understand their causes, we immediately assume that they have been contrived unskilfully. For this reason he stipulated "strenge Kausalität" as the essence of drama (I, 14, 30).

Grillparzer's second play for the popular stage, *Der Traum ein Leben*, shows a dream of a few hours encompassing a whole life-history. When Rustan awakens, he is amazed that his adventures have all happened in a single night, and cries "Eine Nacht? Und war ein Leben" (l. 2618). As in *Die Ahnfrau*, the scene is set at night and the action full of fantastic events which rush on to completion within the limits of the unity of time.

The dream is placed within a framework (Act I and the end of the final Act) during which the dreamer is awake. As we shall see, the use of a framework is common in Grillparzer's plays of action. In this play the framework is a peasant idyll and its function is to make clear why Rustan decides to abandon such a quiet unpretentious existence, the peace of which is brought out by the whole setting of the opening scene—the "ländliche Gegend", the sound of hunting horns and the blinding sun of the summer evening. This framework has but few characters, all serving clear and definite functions. Mirza, Massud and the dervish on the one hand and Zanga on the other represent the two extremes of quiet contentment and restless ambition, the conflict of which torments Rustan. The dervish is never seen but is heard playing his harp at the end of the first and last Acts, and singing his song of renunciation. His introduction shows Rustan's rejection of this philosophy before his dream and his acceptance of it afterwards.

In the dream section of the play it soon becomes apparent that Rustan is ill-suited to the life of adventure for which one part of his being longs. He can rave ecstatically about his new life of freedom (Zanga says to him, roughly, "genug geschwärmt") but is a poor marksman and no soldier. His moral weaknesses are even more apparent. Having been fêted as a hero, he cannot bear to defer to another, as would be necessary if he admitted that the king's escape was not his work. But in taking credit for an action not his own, he is led to experience what (in another connection, see below, p. 51) Grillparzer called, after Schiller, "der Fluch der bösen Tat". An evil deed brings misfortune and to alleviate this, one commits even greater evils. Thus Rustan can only maintain his usurped position by murdering the king's real saviour, and when this crime is discovered he thinks of saving himself by murdering the king. The dream finishes in sheer terror, as Rustan is faced with capture or suicide.

It is this dream section of the play that is filled with exciting action, one violent and surprising development leading to another. The stage is at times crowded, fighting occurs, and the sky is reddened with fire. Not only the swiftness but also the splendour of the action contrasts with the peasant idyll of the framework, and it is, of course, this central section of the play that links it with the Viennese popular stage. It is no coincidence that, of all Grillparzer's plays, this is the one that has long remained most popular in Vienna, and was performed seventy-eight times during his life at the Burgtheater alone.[56, p. xvi]

Although the sequence of events is (by the standards of real life) poorly motivated, there is no artificiality of motivation, since these standards are inappropriate to a nightmare. The behaviour and appearance of the characters in the dream is made to depend on Rustan's waking experience; what we see of this in the opening scenes provides all the elements with which his imagination works in his sleep. Thus the king and the princess are at times reminiscent of Massud and Mirza (Rustan takes Massud and Mirza for them as he awakens), and the man in the brown cloak sometimes looks like Osmin and sometimes behaves as

Osmin had done—as when he tells Rustan: "Rühm dich des, was du getan!" Rustan reacts to the taunt as he did in Act I to Osmin's—by conceding its truth. If the man in the cloak thus represents Rustan's misgivings about himself, the old woman with the goblet equally clearly represents his will to murder the king; she tells him he must accept the inevitable, namely "Eine Leiche, auf dem Thron" (l. 1603).

That the dream projects the craving of Rustan's ambition is pointed out to him by Massud at the end:

> Doch vergiß es nicht, die Träume,
> Sie erschaffen nicht die Wünsche,
> Die vorhandnen wecken sie;
> Und was jetzt verscheucht der Morgen,
> Lag als Keim in dir verborgen. (ll. 2697–2701)

The disastrous outcome of his longing for fame, power and adventure cures Rustan of his ambition, and he awakens to declare that:

> Eines nur ist Glück hienieden,
> Eins, des Innern stiller Frieden,
> Und die schuldbefreite Brust.
> Und die Größe ist gefährlich,
> Und der Ruhm ein leeres Spiel;
> Was er gibt, sind nichtge Schatten,
> Was er nimmt, es ist so viel.

These lines justify Rommel's classification of the play among the "Besserungsstücke" of the Viennese popular stage.[40, p. 819] It is, of course, the hero, not the audience, who is "gebessert". Grillparzer did not think that "all das Leichtfertige und Lustige" that characterizes the theatre makes an appropriate forum for moral teaching, and he insisted that "das Theater muß als sittlich gleichgültig behandelt werden" (II, 8, 180). Nevertheless, Rustan's words represent a standpoint that recurs in other of his plays. We shall meet it again in Medea's final words to Jason and, as Scherer has noted,[42, p. 213] Jason is "der Rustan des Traumes, der aus Ehrgeiz und Ruhmsucht sein Lebensglück in die Schanze geschlagen und sich auf die Bahn des Unrechts begeben hat". The careers of both men illustrate "der Fluch der bösen Tat".

Ottokar is also "der Rustan des Traumes". Grillparzer's heroes (but not his heroines) sacrifice "des Innern stiller Frieden" for the sake of ambition, and in *Sappho* the heroine says that this is essentially a male tendency:

> Gar wechselnd ist des Mannes rascher Sinn (l. 813)
>
> . . . . .
>
> Zu eng dünkt ihm des Innern stille Welt,
> Nach außen geht sein rastlos, wildes Streben. (ll. 819–20)

In the way Grillparzer repeatedly urges the desirability of an unpretentious unassuming life it is possible to see something of the so-called "Biedermeier" phase of German literature, that is (in the late Miss Atkinson's helpful definition), "the comfortable solidity and unenterprising resigned temper of the predominantly middle-class culture that succeeded the age of Romanticism.* Those who accept the Biedermeier values typically lack any ideal for which they would willingly die, and are happy to renounce greatness in return for life. Such an attitude is in part explicable as a reaction against the idealistic heroes of Schiller's dramas, and against the almost superhuman ones of his imitators (Körner's *Zriny* of 1812 typifies their hunger for death and glory). Alternatively, it is possible to regard Grillparzer's standpoint as in some way typically Austrian, since the same ideal is discernible in Raimund and in Stifter. But we shall perhaps be nearer the truth if we regard his attitude as conditioned by his pessimism. His resignation is not an unenterprising withdrawal, but a tragic awareness of how readily tragedy can ensue when any powerful tendency (not only ambition) comes to dominate behaviour. This is the burden of many of his tragedies, and what he stresses in his theory of tragedy, as I shall later show.

2. Ein treuer Diener seines Herrn (1828)

In his autobiography Grillparzer designated the story of Bancbanus as myth rather than history, on the ground that it is told of two men who lived at different times. The facility with

*Ref. 2, p. xxxiii n. For a fuller discussion see ref. 12.

which a story can be transferred from one man to another is in fact a good indication of its mythical nature. Thus one reason why modern historians believe that William Tell never existed is that the incident of the apple-shot had been told of other heroes before the time of his alleged activity. In such cases one looks for a motive for the invention of the narrative. In the case of Bancbanus, Grillparzer interpreted the story as "nichts als eine Einkleidung für die Abneigung der Ungarn gegen die Deutschen" (I, 16, 204). Even the twist that he has given it places the Germans in the worst possible light. The Hungarian king proudly declares:

> Mein Land bewohnt ein einfach stilles Volk,
> Zu jeder Art des Guten rasch und tüchtig. (ll. 293–4)

But the degenerate German Otto von Meran and his sister, the Queen, who weakly pampers him, despise this stolid virtue: "Einfältig Volk! Nur stumpf, nicht tugendhaft" (l. 951). Grillparzer was shocked when the Emperor tried to suppress the play. But one can perhaps understand that the rulers of his multifarious empire, struggling to keep it together against the rising tide of nationalism, would not wish to encourage a work where one of its national groups was played off against another. The authorities had had enough of this in *König Ottokar*, where the Austrians are lauded at the expense of the Czechs.

Weh dem, der lügt! and *Ein treuer Diener* are both problem plays, with the problem indicated in the title and posed in Act I, by the bishop in one case and the king in the other. Once these two characters have stipulated some of the conditions which are to govern the action, they leave the stage, returning only in the final scene to comment on how the problem has been attacked. In both plays, then, the beginning and end, where alone these two characters appear, forms a framework to the rest. And as in *Der Traum ein Leben*, the frame consists of a slow-moving exposition and conclusion, while the main body is full of swift and exciting developments.

Grillparzer felt that he had overdone the emphasis on action in the central section of *Ein treuer Diener*. He wrote: "Ich fand das Stück viel zu roh und gewalttätig" (*ibid.*, p. 206)—although he also said (in a diary entry of 1828) that poets ought sometimes to aim at theatrical effects so that the public shall realize that their normal absence from poetic works is not due to incapacity (II, 8, 293).

The opening Act draws the characters of Bancbanus and Otto (complete opposites in appearance as well as character) and the king and queen. Bancbanus is on the stage for most of the play, except in Act III, where his wife Erny is driven to her death. He is not a hero who is meant to fill us with enthusiasm—Grillparzer himself called him "ein ziemlich bornierter alter Mann" (I, 16, 204) —but he never forfeits our sympathy. In the opening scene his pedantry would verge on the ridiculous if it did not show that he alone of his friends and enemies can remain calm under provocation. Both the opening scenes illustrate his "Gleichmut"—a quality which infuriates Otto and is brought out by contrast with the duke's own "Toben" (ll. 152–3; cf. l. 1034).

The king is about to lead his army to war and appoints Bancbanus regent to act with his queen during his absence, saying as he confers the powers upon him: "Stets warst du treuer Diener deines Herrn" (l. 382). Bancbanus is charged to keep peace in the realm, but he cannot inculcate in others the loyalty to the king's most unjust family by which he is himself inspired. If he is "borniert" it is his almost servile respect for the royal family that makes him so, not the means he adopts to serve them and to combine this service with maintaining the peace. Although they mock him, he will allow no one to disrespect them. When a farmer whose corn has been ruined by Otto and his huntsmen indicts the duke, Bancbanus insists that the charge be brought against the whole company, not against the duke alone.

> Wo bleibt die Achtung,
> Verwünschtes Volk, für eurer Fürstin Bruder? (ll. 548–9)

Whenever he alone is the victim, he will endure any wrong from the queen or from Otto. In the very first scene he shuts his eyes to the fact that Otto is among the jesters outside his window and refuses to listen to reports about the duke's misbehaviour. When

Erny, his wife, cries "Scham und Schmach" as he is held up to ridicule, he retorts:

> Nur eine Schmach weiß ich auf dieser Erde,
> Und die heißt: Unrecht tun! (ll. 83–4)

He is, then, convinced that to suffer injustice is not shameful. Grillparzer designates his attitude as "Heroismus der Pflichttreue" (I, 16, 204) and Scherer finds him reminiscent of the heroes of Jesuit drama who reaffirm their beliefs under any temptation or torture.[42, p. 250] But although he will suffer anything for himself, in the course of the play he has to decide to what extent he must insist on like conduct from his own family. His counsel on this matter is reasonable, although the circumstances are such as to provoke unreason in anyone not capable of the utter selflessness that characterizes him. It is certainly not in the nature of his family to act on his dispassionate and far-sighted advice.

The king's mildness of character lays the basis of the whole tragedy, and also makes his final clemency intelligible and plausible. His judgement is often warped by his affections. He assures Bancbanus that the queen is "gerecht und klug" immediately after she has lied to him in order to achieve her will, and then given a public display of petulance when she failed to do so! He very nearly gives in to her request that Otto be appointed regent, although he is quite aware of Otto's lack of "Sitte" (l. 279) and must surely see that the doting way in which she says she will control him (ll. 303–8) means that she will in fact be quite powerless to exercise this control. In putting Bancbanus in charge, but at the same time doing nothing to curb Otto, he is creating a situation fraught with danger, for Bancbanus' finest qualities provoke Otto beyond endurance. It is annoyance at Bancbanus' superlative self-control rather than any real interest in Erny, whose coldness he professes to disdain, that makes Otto pursue her (ll. 182–5).

From the beginning of Act II the action becomes progressively more exciting, the language more colloquial and with noticeably fewer images. Images retard the action while one thing is likened to or equated with another, and so it is not surprising that there are few of them where action is developed quickly. Altogether, the language of this play is much more colloquial than is usual with Grillparzer. Erny, for instance, indicates her own character by saying: "Mein Vater sprach wohl oft: Sie hats im Nacken!" (l. 665). And Bancbanus repeatedly introduces his remarks with a "nu, nu" or "i nu".

Bancbanus appears at the beginning of this second Act with his nose buried in a sheaf of documents, talking of wills and codicils, fumbling for his papers, not even noticing that the queen has terminated the meeting he thinks he is addressing and has sent everyone away. Even the servants mock him, and in this Act we see how much in the play consists of comic motifs turned to tragic account; the old man with the young wife; and the pedantic prosaic civil servant who is derided at court. But his pedantry does not spring from stupidity. It seems an almost deliberate expression of his determination not to allow derision to deflect him from what he sees as his duty.

When he first hears that Otto is importuning his wife at the dance, he is confident that she can deal with the situation without his intervention (l. 596), and sends her back to this festival that it is her duty, as the regent's wife, to attend (ll. 630–1). But he cannot know at this juncture that Otto has some hold over her. Grillparzer conceived Otto as a man who would not relentlessly pursue a woman who had shown no interest in him, and we learn that she once, innocently enough, gave a token of her favour —thinking at that time (before she had come to know him well) that he was "fromm und gut" (l. 774)—and that Otto, used as he is to captivating women, has interpreted this as a major passion which she is trying to suppress. The dialogue between the two in which all this is revealed gave Grillparzer great difficulty, and he rewrote it many times.[41, p. 12] When Bancbanus learns from her something of the truth, he realizes at once he must, after all, take her from the court as soon as an acceptable pretext can be found. All that he requires of her is to behave with restraint in the meantime (ll. 887–9). She, however, is no Bancbanus, and turns on Otto with words of undisguised contempt (l. 898).

From this point Otto is primarily concerned with her, and no longer merely using her as a means for provoking Bancbanus to anger. Grillparzer noted that Otto's fundamental trait of character is "Übermuth"; he has always had his own way and has always been a favourite with women. Now suddenly he is faced not merely with rejection but with open contempt, and it is more than he can stand. The catastrophic effect on him of Erny's words is clear not only from his immediate reaction to them, but also from his physical collapse in Act III, which is represented as following the shock of the insult. Erny's indiscretion is underlined by contrast with the words of the king in Act I. He also despises Otto, but avoids saying so explicitly even to his queen, let alone to Otto himself. When the queen says: "Ihr liebt ihn nicht", he replies: "Ich liebe, was ich achte" (l. 252). Erny might have known that a spoiled prince would react violently to an insult, but her disdain is quite in accordance with her wilful impetuous character. As Bancbanus says, she is headstrong ("ruschlich", l. 1376), and the tragedy arises because she cannot accept what he can.

When at the end of Act III Otto calls in his men and orders them to seize her, she reacts with her usual forcefulness and impetuosity—by stabbing herself to death. The way Grillparzer avoids rhetoric in this play is well illustrated when Bancbanus seeing her dead, expresses his grief in a single line. Grillparzer was consciously resisting the taste of the age in replacing rhetoric with action: "Sie sind auf ihrem Theater an den prächtigen Wortschwall gewohnt; die Handlung mit unbedeckter Blöße ärgert ihr keusches Auge" (II, 8, 296).

Grillparzer's next problem was to motivate Bancbanus' failure to avenge Erny. He knows nothing of the circumstances that led to her death, and although he naturally suspects Otto, he fears that her own impetuosity may have been partly to blame. His hesitation is increased when the queen, in order to protect Otto, says that she killed Erny to punish her for a misdemeanour. In consequence, an inquiry into what actually happened can be instigated only by the king, and Bancbanus decides he must await his master's return and in the meantime at all costs keep the peace, as he has promised. But his brother Peter and his brother-in-law Simon demand that the queen hand Otto into their safe custody until the king returns. They know that unless they secure Otto's person, she will contrive his escape from the country. Bancbanus realizes that this is in fact what will happen, but that the rational course is for them all to suffer it. If Erny's life could still be saved, he would agree to forceful measures (1. 1398). But to threaten the queen as things are would be unwarranted rebellion, with civil war as an inevitable consequence if she refuses to comply.

When the queen rejects their demand, Simon and Peter prepare to attack the palace and secure Otto. But Bancbanus cannot allow the queen and her young child, the nation's future king, to be exposed to the dangers of a siege. Thus his conception of duty and loyalty, which has kept him inactive up to this point, now forces him into action against his own family. The siege takes place: the queen makes Bancbanus save Otto as a condition of being allowed to save her and the child. Otto and the child escape but the queen is killed by Peter, who thinks he is aiming at Otto. That it is Peter who has killed his queen is another tragic feature, for of all the rebels he is least convinced that rebellion is justified. And her death is not a contingency that spoils the effectiveness of the tragedy, for it is not unjust. She had protected Otto by taking responsibility for his crime, and she is made to atone for the guilt she thus took upon herself. Hence Bancbanus can say (1. 2002) that her death, though accidental, was an act of divine retribution.

As Act V opens Otto, who is completely silent, follows Bancbanus and the child to safety. When Bancbanus thinks of him as Erny's killer, he addresses him as "Mörder", but when he is conscious that he must rely on him to save the child he respectfully calls him "Herzog". The alternation between these two appellations brings out the conflict in his mind which constitutes the poignancy of this scene.

Finally he bids Otto flee with the child, and Grillparzer contrives to make us fear for a while that further drastic developments may occur. But the rebellion collapses at the return of the king, who recognizes how much misfortune has stemmed from his failure to curb Otto. Here Grillparzer's striking imagery returns to the play, and the emphasis is no longer on action, but on comment and reflection:

> Unsittlichkeit! Du allgefräßger Krebs,
> Du Wurm an alles Wohlseins tiefsten Wurzeln,
> Du Raupe an des Staates Lebensmark!
> Warum ließ ich beim Scheiden dich zurück?
> Warum zertrat ich nicht, verwies dich?
> Wie schlecht verwahrtes Feuer gingst du auf
> Und fraßest all mein Haus, mein Heil, mein Glück!
>
> (ll. 1919–25)

He asks Bancbanus "Wo ist mein Weib?", knowing full well that she is dead and asking the question only in order to imply that Bancbanus has not been a "treuer Diener". Bancbanus' reply is a complete answer and also expresses a pathetic sarcasm:

> Daß Gott! die kehrte heim.
> Sie wollte sehn, wie's meinem Weib erging!

The effectiveness of the central Acts derives from their remorseless action, meticulously motivated. Only in this final Act do we meet such pathos. Bancbanus here expresses his grief and shows himself wiser than the rebels in words which are profoundly moving. His tragedy is that he is made to serve masters who are worsened by his very rectitude, and that when they have thus inspired hatred and contempt he can control these emotions in himself but cannot bring others to act with like restraint. He concludes the play with an appeal to the future monarch, the child he has saved:

> Sei mild, du Fürstenkind, und sei gerecht!
> Auf dem Gerechten ruht des Herren Segen.
> Bezähm dich selbst, nur wer sich selbst bezähmt
> Mag des Gesetzes scharfe Zügel lenken.
> Laß dir den Menschen Mensch sein, und den Diener
> Acht als ein Spargut für die Zeit der Not.

Grillparzer did not think the theatre should be used for preaching morality, and the reflections with which he often concludes his plays do not serve this purpose, but enable us calmly to survey the often tumultuous action that has preceded, and somehow sum it up in words of tranquillity.

3. Weh dem, der lügt! (1838)

Der Traum ein Leben was a great success on the Viennese stage in 1834. When it became known in 1838 that Grillparzer was to put on another play, a comedy, expectations ran high and for this very reason were easily disappointed. The play failed at its first performance, and Grillparzer was so embittered that he withheld the remaining three dramas he subsequently completed (*Ein Bruderzwist in Habsburg, Die Jüdin von Toledo* and *Libussa*) from publication in his lifetime.

The failure of the comedy was partly his own fault, for he insisted on advertising it as a "Lustspiel"; so the audience was expecting something uproariously funny, like the clowning they were used to in the popular theatres of the city.* But although the play is an effective comedy, there is nothing hilarious, and it is not until well into the first Act that Grillparzer even attempts to raise a smile—by making Leon the cook tell the bishop he must eat better, since:

> Ihr müßt dereinst am jüngsten Tag vertreten
> Wohl Eure Seel, ich Euern Leib von Rechtens. (ll. 221-2)

But immediately after this mild joke the conversation again becomes deadly earnest, as Leon tells his first lie and is met by the bishop's sharp "Weh dem, der lügt!" followed by a theological tirade, partly in rhymed verse as befits the elevated theme:

> Was weißt du schwacher Wurm von Zweck und Enden?
> Der oben wirds zu seinem Ziele wenden.
> Du sollst die Wahrheit reden, frecher Bursch. (ll. 250-2)

When the bishop first appears he is soliloquizing over his sermon notes, and what he says has justly been called a homily. Grillparzer himself attributed the failure of the play partly to his having put a sermon on the stage.†

The unsuccessful first performance was also due to the fact that the character of Galomir was felt to be overdrawn. Grillparzer

---

*See Laube's comments of 1872, quoted by Waterhouse.[51, p. xxvi]
†See Kataan.[21, p. 200]

observed that the actor who played the part "glaubte ihn gar nicht genug als Idioten, als Cretin halten zu können". Grillparzer's own interpretation of the role is open to objection. He wrote in his diary for 1839 that:

> Galomir ist so wenig dumm, als die Thiere dumm sind; sie denken nur nicht. Galomir kann darum nicht sprechen weil er auch nicht denkt; das würde ihn aber nicht hindern, z.B. in der Schlacht den rechten Angriffspunkt instinktmäßig recht gut herauszufinden. Er ist thierisch, aber nicht blödsinnig. (II, 10, 290.)

It is strange that a man of Grillparzer's insight should suggest that lack of ideas will necessarily shut a man's mouth, and that animals are incapable of reflection.*

Another cause of failure was that Atalus appeared to the aristocracy in the audience as a caricature of themselves. Almost everything he says when we first meet him in Act II expresses his snobbishness. He despises Leon for being a cook; he will woo Edrita only if his king confers a patent of nobility upon her family; and he is prepared to mind a horse, "ein edles ritterliches Thier", whereas to work in the kitchen would be to disgrace his family name. Aristocrats in German comedy have had an interesting history; Gottsched (who insisted on having them in tragedy) banished them from comedy because he equated it with ridicule, and to laugh derisively at aristocrats was out of the question. Lessing brought them back in his *Minna von Barnhelm*, but treated them seriously and sympathetically. The characters one laughs at in this play are, apart from the foreigner Riccaut, all bourgeois— the landlord, for instance, who like most innkeepers in comedy is avaricious and anxious to pry into other people's business.

---

*He inveighed often enough against empty verbiage: "Der Deutsche ist von der Schule her gewohnt, mit Verachtung des gesunden Menschenverstandes sich mit Worten zu begnügen, die in den Adelsstand der Begriffe erhoben werden" (II, 11, 103). He also stated that emotion (certainly displayed by animals) is fundamentally akin to thought (II, 9, 19), and that man's advantage lies not so much in the superiority of his mental processes, as in his capacity to profit from the accumulated knowledge that reaches him as tradition, whereas the individual ape of every generation has to begin the process of discovery anew (II, 8, 180 and II, 12, 39).

Grillparzer was perhaps taking a risk when he dared to make an aristocrat look ridiculous.

Laube, who produced most of Grillparzer's plays successfully in the 1850's, did not touch this one, and thought it "eine geistvolle literarische Arbeit", but not "ein wirksames Theaterstück". (51, p. xxvi) Yet it does in fact contain many elements which make for effectiveness on the stage. It is based on an original idea (the hero gains his end by invariably telling the truth) and contains amusing situations, such as Leon's antics in the kitchen and Galomir's fall into the moat. The contrast between the cultured Franks and the unnamed barbarians east of the Rhine is expressed wittily in terms of culinary skills and interests, and Grillparzer handles this theme in such a way as to suggest that he is contrasting the French and the Germans. Also, he invented Edrita, who was no part of his source material, so as to increase the interest with a minor love motif. Finally, the action is made as exciting and as swift as possible. The danger of the rescue bid is repeatedly underlined, and it is made more difficult by the passive resistance of Atalus. The plot is developed swiftly without loss of plausibility, for the conspirators are given motives for immediate action. Edrita is to be married on the morrow, and Leon and Atalus will then be separated; so the two must escape at once or never.

The swift action is placed in a frame (Act I and the end of the final Act) just as in *Der Traum ein Leben* and *Ein treuer Diener*. The bishop appears only in the frame; he sets the problem (to rescue Atalus without lying) and returns at the end to be told how it was accomplished. He is off-stage long enough for us to accept his final change of attitude. In comedy the upsets portrayed are essentially remediable and this is certainly the case here. Not only is Atalus released from his captivity, so that the bishop need grieve no more for him, but also the bishop himself is finally cured of his moral rigorism. In Act I he would rather let his nephew suffer injustice than lie in order to prevent this. And even if the lad is treated so badly that he dies, then let him die, rather than any lie be told to save his life and restore his freedom (1. 345). By the final Act, however, he has come to see that absolute veracity

is out of the question in this "buntverworrene Welt". He told
Leon at the outset that the trust and confidence which man places
in man is undermined by lying. But even by persistently telling
the truth Leon finds that he disappoints the confidence which his
enemies placed in him. Edrita argues that by disappointing their
expectations of him he has in fact lied to them. She subscribes not
only to the bishop's proposition that lying destroys confidence,
but also to the further view that everything which destroys confidence is a lie. She says:

> Es lügt der Mensch mit Worten nicht allein,
> Auch mit der Tat. Sprachst du die drohnde Wahrheit,
> Und wir, wir haben dennoch dir vertraut,
> War Lüge denn, was dir *erwarb* Vertrauen.*

If this principle be accepted, then Leon is both a liar and a thief.
By his very adherence to the abstract principle of absolute
veracity he has stolen Edrita's heart (see her accusation, l. 1798)
and raised her hopes of his love only to dash them (ll. 1330–5).
So Leon has not been honest, although he could not have been
more honest. The bishop draws the obvious inference at the end
when he admits that the ethical ideal he so confidently proclaimed
is proper to God rather than to man, who must be content to live
by a less exalted code:

> Das Unkraut, merk ich, rottet man nicht aus,
> Glück auf, wächst nur der Weizen etwa drüber. (ll. 1805–6).

Grillparzer is poking fun at absolute veracity, just as Lessing had
mocked Tellheim's exaggerated sense of honour in *Minna von
Barnhelm*. This critical attitude to absolute standards is what we
should expect from Grillparzer's comedy, just as in his tragedies
he reacts against Schiller's heroes, who rigidly adhere to their
idealistic principles.

In the legend as told by Gregory of Tour's *Historia Francorum*
there is no promise by Leon to tell the truth, but he does, on one
occasion, tell his captor Kattwald that he intends to escape.
Grillparzer was obviously struck by this incident and was led to

---

*Lines 1137–40 of the first edition. See I, 5, 372 f.

invent a plot in which Leon's telling the truth was to be the condition under which alone he was to be allowed to try to free
Atalus. To explain the imposition of this condition Grillparzer
had to make the bishop initially a rigorist who prohibits lying
absolutely. And to motivate the acceptance of the bishop's
condition, he skilfully made Leon a frank and open fellow, who
begins the play by calling his master to account, and demanding
that he justify his apparent miserliness.

Since this ethical problem became the basis of his treatment of
the material, Grillparzer produced a very elevated comedy.
Gregor, helpless to save his nephew and determined not to have
him freed by lying, cries:

> Du Vater Aller,
> In deine Hand befehl ich meinen Sohn! (ll. 333–4)

This is very pious and Christian, but not exactly what one expects
from a comedy, and in fact Grillparzer has ennobled the facts of
his sources in many ways. His Leon is the free servant, not the
slave of the bishop. Only the "barbarians" beyond (i.e. east of)
the Rhine, who murder Christian missionaries (as we are told by
Edrita, ll. 1151 4), keep slaves, and so Leon can be sold into
captivity among them. The bishop is also represented as incapable
of persecuting. At the end he invites the barbarians to join the
Church, but adds "Hier ist kein Zwang" (l. 1728). This picture of
these early Christians as refined and gracious pietists has led some
to denounce the play as mere Romantic nonsense—as if Grillparzer
had tried to give a historically accurate portrait. However, that
he does idealize makes his comedy very different from most, as
we can see if we compare it with Kleist's *Der Zerbrochene Krug*.
In this comedy of lies the personal happiness of Eve and Ruprecht
is threatened, and Eve's grief that Ruprecht is unable to trust
her is genuinely tragic. But the stress is not upon such serious
matters, but upon trivialities, such as the jug and its history, and
much of the humour consists in punning and word-play. The
characters are unimportant people who take small matters
seriously. Grillparzer's characters, however, include a bishop and

a Christian who seriously tries to practise an exalted ideal. And the ethical problem is discussed in long monologues (the bishop's in Act I and Leon's in Act V). This seriousness is not lightened by any form of word-play, and the absence of this feature is particularly striking in view of Grillparzer's close relation to Raimund and other writers of the Viennese popular stage.

Grillparzer's idealizing tendency has nothing to do with religious proselytizing. Apart from the fact that he was the last person to write pious stories from religious zeal,* he has even deleted the miracles on which the successful escape was made to depend in his sources. In the legend, the gate is opened by divine intervention to allow Leon and Atalus to escape. With Grillparzer, it is Edrita who supplies the key. In this play Grillparzer uses the miraculous exactly as he used fate in *Die Ahnfrau*. He realized that the audiences to which he was appealing believed neither in fate as a supernatural, malignant power, nor in a Deity who works miracles in order to cure the minor difficulties of Christians. But he knew that modern man does nevertheless half-believe in fate and in a miracle-working Deity, and that this belief can be played on. The dramatist must not include any action or event that is interpretable only as a miracle and is inexplicable on any other basis, for, as Grillparzer said concerning the idea of fate, "ein ausgesprochener Irrtum stößt zurück" (I, 14, 18). Consequently, he deleted all the miracles in the source materials and invented a number of incidents which suggest miraculous intervention (if we are inclined to believe in it) but which we can explain naturally. Thus, when Leon makes his pact with the bishop, the latter tells him that God will succour him. Leon falls on his knees crying "es blitzte". And Gregor comments: "Im Innern hat des Guten Geist geleuchet" (l. 381). In Act V Leon recalls this incident:

> ich bitte, Herr! [God]
> Als ich von deinem frommen Diener schied,
> Da leuchtete ein Blitz in meinem Innern;
> Von Wundern sprachs, ein Wunder soll geschehn.
>
> (ll. 1682–6)

---

*For his attitude to Catholic miracles and ritual see ref. 20, pp. 14 ff.

and then he finds that the Christians have captured Metz the previous day and so are there to save them. Both incidents suggest the miraculous, without actual proof that would commit the dramatist to it or make the effectiveness of the play dependent on readiness to believe in it. The same is true of the scene in Act IV where Kattwald's vassal, the ferryman, is told that the fugitives are friends of his master and that he should therefore put them across the river. But Leon intervenes with the truth, tells him that they are Kattwald's enemies, whereupon the ferryman (who has a secret grudge against his master) makes haste to save them. The words "dankt dem droben" (l. 1546) suggest that their rescue here is due to divine assistance, and this impression is reinforced by much kneeling and praying to a sacred image throughout this scene. But again, there is no proof of miracle and the events can be explained quite naturally. Grillparzer surely deliberately left the reader to think what he liked here, as he did apropos of fate in *Die Ahnfrau*.

CHAPTER 2

THE GREEK TRAGEDIES

1. Sappho (1818)

In the draft of a letter to Müllner of 1818, Grillparzer confessed to being somewhat ashamed of what he called the "tolles Treiben" in *Die Ahnfrau,* and was anxious to show that he could write a play without bangs and ghosts. He added that when he came across the story of Sappho, he realized at once that he had found the material he needed for a calm play with a simple plot (III, 1. 97).

The simplicity of the material enabled him to keep the three unities. This is in fact the only play of his which keeps the unity of place; as a result, direct action is curtailed and messengers are brought on to narrate what has happened. Thus, in the first scene, Rhamnes tells the slave-girls what Sappho has achieved during her absence. The way Sappho and Phaon became acquainted is conveyed entirely by Phaon's narrative (I, 3); Eucharis narrates what happened at the banquet (between Acts I and II) at which Melitta and Phaon first become conscious of each other and which serves, as Grillparzer said, "sie in jenen Zustand des Berührtseyns zu bringen, das der Liebe den Weg bereitet" (*ibid.,* p. 101). Eucharis also narrates Melitta's ablutions (II, 3), the return of Melitta and Phaon as captives (V, 1) and—most important of all—Sappho's august behaviour (V, 5) before her final entry. Since Grillparzer prefers direct action to narrative, he does not, in his later plays, keep the unity of place, which has messengers' reports as a natural concomitant. Even in *Sappho* a great deal is directly enacted: e.g. the scene culminating in Phaon kissing Melitta, which is witnessed by Sappho, who tries to convince herself that nevertheless all is well; also the scenes where Phaon speaks Melitta's name in his dream, and Sappho, although she still resists the obvious inference, decides to question the girl; when she does so, her anger is thoroughly aroused, and she draws her knife. All these scenes bring direct and swift action.

Grillparzer did not find it easy to make his material into a convincing tragedy. In antiquity Sappho's story had been the theme of comedies. It was the comic poets who linked her with Phaon, who is not mentioned in any of her extant poems. In these comedies he is an ugly old ferryman, rejuvenated by magic ointment, supplied by Aphrodite, and then in consequence pestered by women, of whom Sappho is one. Because of her age her advances evoke no response, so she throws herself from the rock at the end of the isle of Leucas. Tradition prescribed such behaviour to cure the pangs of unrequited love; the victim jumped in, was taken from the water, and could go on repeating the jump until well and truly "cooled off" in every respect.

Grillparzer had to avoid what Carlyle called "the ridicule that lies within a single step of Sappho's tragic situation."[7, p. 332] An oldish woman pursuing a young man could well be represented as ridiculous. Grillparzer himself seems to have felt that such material is repulsive rather than comic:

> Sappho ist in der Katastrophe [viz. Act IV] ein verliebtes, eifersüchtiges, in der Leidenschaft sich vergessendes Weib; ein Weib, das einen *jüngern* Mann liebt. In der gewöhnlichen Welt ist ein solches Weib ein ekelhafter Gegenstand. (III, 1, 99.)

Scherer asserts that the comic element shows through the action of Grillparzer's play, and also that "die Gestalt der Sappho im Ganzen hat etwas unwillkürlich zur Parodie Herausforderndes." [42, p. 234] He is thinking in particular of her suicidal leap from the rock, and says we do not feel that her passion was so great that she cannot go on living. But we must ask whether it is her passion for Phaon that in fact motivates her suicide, or whether the text gives other reasons for her behaviour. As Rippman notes, most critics have found the final tragic outcome unconvincing.

He himself asserts that we "cannot but feel that death is the true ending".[38, p. xii] But the question is: what is the basis for this feeling, if in fact we have it?

From what we are told in Act I it seems that Sappho felt desperately in need of a partner. Her relationship with Phaon was begun at the Olympic festival entirely on her initiative. He was standing "schamentgeistert" in her presence, and she bade him follow her (l. 253). He is still bewildered when they arrive in Lesbos at the beginning of the play (ll. 317–18). Her view of him then is naïvely ideal—she even recommends him to her people as an accomplished poet (l. 77)! From the first she is unsure of his affection. She warns him that she will be capable of any unreasonable behaviour if he becomes indifferent to her (ll. 123–7). And when he expresses his ecstatic feelings, she replies that he may one day view her more realistically and therefore less favourably (ll. 202–3). The basis for her fears is that she has become embittered by painful disappointments in friendship and love, and also by the early death of her family (ll. 113–22), whereas Phaon is young and a complete stranger to the cynicism born of disappointment. It is surely because of her loneliness and unhappiness that she was drawn to him in the first place, and thus deludes herself into thinking that his admiration of her is love. She expressly contrasts her own bitterness with his "Lebenslust" and "Lust an dem, was ist" (ll. 265, 267), and a little later she elaborates this contrast (ll. 370–92) and designates it as the "gulf" which divides them (l. 394). She begs the gods to give her back the outlook of her youth (ll. 380–7) and so bring her into harmony with him. But it is obviously impossible for her to become young again, "mit runden Kinderwangen", as she charmingly puts it, and the relationship is soon terminated. But this hardly gives her a motive for suicide. It would be unconvincing if she were finally to think that she cannot live without this callow youth who lacks intellectual interests and never loved her anyway. It is quite plausible that, in her state of lonely unhappiness, she should have fallen in love with him; but by the end of the play she has realized that he could never have understood her (l. 1962) and that they had better part. Nor is she represented as killing herself because, in the grief of her recent disappointment, she despairs of finding any suitable partner, yet feels she cannot live without one.

We must look for other clues. After she has spoken of the difference in age and outlook between herself and Phaon and called it the "gulf" which lies between them, she immediately goes on to describe this gulf in very different terms, and it is not easy to see the connection between her two interpretations of it. The second of these is that in pursuing her literary ambitions she has become cut off from normal warm human contacts:

> Weh Dem, den aus der Seinen stillem Kreise
> Des Ruhms, der Ehrsucht eitler Schatten lockt. (ll. 398–9)

She goes on to liken such a person to a mariner sailing through rough seas in a light boat. He has no green fields nor flowers, nor any living thing around him, but only the grey limitless expanses of the sea. The coast which harbours his loved ones he only sees afar off, and their cries are drowned by the roar of the waves. When he does finally return, the flowers are dead, and all life and warmth has gone. Although this whole extended simile expresses the lot of anyone who neglects those closest to him in his pursuit of his ambition, Sappho is, of course, thinking primarily of literary ambition and fame. She has just won a laurel wreath at the Olympic competition, but this success seems to her as barren as the laurel leaves. In an earlier scene she had made similar remarks:

> Umsonst nicht hat zum Schmuck der Musen Chor
> Den unfruchtbaren Lorbeer sich erwählt,
> Kalt, frucht- und duftlos drücket er das Haupt
> Dem er Ersatz versprach für manches Opfer. (ll. 271–4)

It is not that she has been unhappy all her life; her single-minded devotion to literary composition has brought her "des Vollbringens Wahnsinnglühende Lust" (l. 50). But she wants the warmth of family life instead, and fears that, like the mariner in her image, she will find only desolation on returning to land. In sum, then, the gulf between herself and Phaon exists (1) because of her maturity and bitterness of outlook and (2) because she has pursued her (literary) ambition instead of cultivating human relationships. She feels strongly that to devote herself further to literature would be incompatible with marriage, and so she proposes now to live a simple unpretentious life with Phaon and renounce all her ambition. She says to her people:

> An seiner Seite werd' ich unter euch
> Ein einfach stilles Hirtenleben führen.   (ll. 93–4)

She will not give up her art altogether, but will

> Zum Preise nur von häuslich stillen Freuden
> Die Töne wecken dieses Saitenspiels.

So at this stage she believes that she can reconcile art and life (cf. ll. 280–3), although only by restricting her art drastically.

The view of poetry which she takes in Act I (clear from the passage where she specifies the dire consequences of ambition) is due partly to the fact that she is full of her love and of the married happiness that she thinks awaits her. When her relationship with Phaon has gone badly wrong, she exaggerates in the opposite direction. Instead of the argument of Act I (that devotion to literary ambition has brought her barren recompense) she says in Act IV that she was happy enough in the "meadows of poetry" until Phaon destroyed her composure. Here, it is poetry that is associated with flowers and fields, and the laurel wreath is designated not "dürr", but "heiter" (ll. 1272 ff.).

Grillparzer's comments on the play give some guidance as to how Sappho's position as an artist is related to her personal tragedy, although they do not appear completely consistent. Sometimes he suggests that her tragedy is due to her personal character, while on other occasions he derives it from the fact that she is an artist. The former view is stated in his autobiography, where he says it was not his intention to stress the poetess in Sappho:

> Ich war nämlich immer ein Feind der Künstlerdramen. Künstler sind gewohnt, die Leidenschaft als einen Stoff zu behandeln. Dadurch wird auch die wirkliche Liebe für sie mehr eine Sache der Imagination als der tiefen Empfindung. Ich wollte aber Sappho einer wahren Leidenschaft, und nicht einer Verirrung der Phantasie zum Opfer werden lassen. (I, 16, 130–1.)

He specifies how the tragedy is derived from Sappho's character in the draft of the letter to Müllner, saying that she is:

> ein Charakter, der Sammelplatz glühender Leidenschaften, über die aber eine *erworbene* Ruhe, die schöne Frucht höherer Geistesbildung, den Szepter führt, bis die angeschmiedeten Sklaven [viz. her passions] die Ketten brechen und dastehen und Wuth schnauben. (III, 1, 97.)

The text certainly confirms this view of Sappho's character. She warns Phaon in Act I:

> Du kennst noch nicht die Unermeßlichkeit,
> Die auf und nieder wogt in dieser Brust.   (ll. 126–7)

In conversation with Melitta a little later she confesses to such unpleasant traits as "der Stolz, die Ehrbegier, des Zornes Stachel" (l. 350), and it is clear that she has been quick-tempered and hurtful to the girl on occasions (ll. 359–60). Melitta herself concedes that her mistress is "heftig manchmal, rasch und bitter" (l. 671). And in Act IV, when Phaon and Melitta have aroused Sappho's rage, she begs the gods to protect her from the violence of her own passions:

> Beschützt mich, Götter, schützt mich vor mir selber!
> Des Innern düstre Geister wachen auf
> Und rütteln an des Kerkers Eisenstäben!   (ll. 1219–22)

This image is exactly how Grillparzer expresses himself in the letter to Müllner, where he speaks of her "enchained" passions bursting their bonds. Sappho, then, reaches a tragic situation because she is an unbalanced woman, easily led astray by rage and jealousy.

However, Grillparzer added to the words last quoted from the letter to Müllner:

> Dazu [viz. in addition to Sappho's character] gesellte sich, sobald das Wort: *Dichterin* einmal ausgesprochen war, natürlich auf der Stelle der Kontrast zwischen Kunst und Leben (wenn die Ahnfrau unwillkürlich gewissermaßen eine Paraphrase des berüchtigten d'Alembert'schen malheur d'être geworden ist, so dürfte wohl die Sappho ein in eben dem Sinne wahres malheur d'être poète in sich fassen).

He goes on to say that Phaon and Melitta represent life ("haben die Parthie des Lebens"), and that he was trying to depict "nicht die Mißgunst, das Ankämpfen des Lebens gegen die Kunst, . . . wie in Corregio oder Tasso, sondern die natürliche Scheidewand, die zwischen beiden befestigt ist". We have seen that one reason given in the text to explain the existence of this "natural barrier" is that devotion to art cuts the poet off from family life. But Sappho is prepared to abandon (or at any rate drastically restrict) her art in order to devote herself to her husband, and there is nothing in the text to suggest that she would have been incapable of finding happiness in this way if she had been given the chance. It seems that we must look for another reason for the poet's unhappiness—one that also links up with Sappho's character as an unbalanced woman.

Douglas Yates has made some helpful suggestions on this head. (55, pp. 35–6) He shows it was Grillparzer's opinion that the artist has violent passions of which he easily loses control. Thus Grillparzer once observed that he himself had strong passions, and that the dramatist must have them (and try to control them in his life) in order to depict them in his plays. Yates also points to a passage in the letter to Müllner that supports this interpretation. Grillparzer there says that Sappho has a "Kraft" (as a poetess) "die mit unter die erregenden Kräfte des Sturms [der Leidenschaft] selber gehört". This clearly implies that her nature as a poetess is partly responsible for her passionate outburst in Act IV, where her "erworbene Ruhe" vanishes and gives way to "Wut".

Yates' theory enables us to understand the basis of Sappho's behaviour up to the beginning of Act V. But at the end of this final Act, she adopts a new and unexpected attitude, claiming to have "found herself" (l. 1960). What exactly does this mean? Yates thinks that the idea is that the artist is something priestly, even divine, not to be sullied by contact with what is merely human; and that she is now conscious of having betrayed her art by wanting to marry and enjoy life. As Yates himself is aware, this is very different from the theory that the artist is an uncontrolled person who cannot cope with life because of his passions.

Now is it in fact the case that Sappho thinks, in Act V or elsewhere, that she has betrayed her art? She does seem to express this idea in Act III, when her relationship with Phaon has begun to deteriorate radically. In this Act she has (like the priest in Act IV of *Des Meeres und der Liebe Wellen*) a number of monologues in which she resists believing something that she knows at heart to be true. When finally she can no longer resist the conviction that Phaon has betrayed her, she denounces herself for renouncing her art and seeking happiness with a mere mortal:

> O Törin! Warum stieg ich von den Höhn,
> Die Lorbeer krönt, wo Aganippe rauscht,
> Mit Sternenklang sich Musenchöre gatten,
> Hernieder in das engbegrenzte Tal,
> Wo Armut herrscht und Treubruch und Verbrechen?
> Dort oben war mein Platz, dort an den Wolken,
> Hier ist kein Ort für mich, als nur das Grab.
> Wen Götter sich zum Eigentum erlesen,
> Geselle sich zu Erdenbürgern nicht,
> Der Menschen und der Überird's chen Los
> Es mischt sich nimmer in demselben Becher.   (ll. 942–52)

In what follows she certainly does not act on this conviction that she has kinship with the gods and not with man; for instead of transcending her own all-too-human nature, she goes on to reveal jealousy and vindictiveness in her resolve to summon Melitta in order to see why such an empty-headed girl could have impressed Phaon (ll. 963 ff.). When the girl comes, Sappho even draws a dagger on her. Then in Act IV she reaches her lowest moral level. In her opening monologue she convinces herself that ingratitude is a worse crime than murder. The implication is that Phaon (guilty of ingratitude to her) is worse than she (a potential murderess in her behaviour towards Melitta). She decides to take vengeance on Melitta by banishing her to Chios where she will suffer the pangs of unrequited love (ll. 1239–41). In scene 2 she continues to vent her fury at Phaon's ingratitude and orders Rhamnes to remove Melitta by trickery or by actual violence if necessary (l. 1322). When Phaon foils this scheme and himself takes flight with the girl, Sappho breathes "nur Wut und Rache!" (l. 1531), and is so utterly exhausted by the emotional turmoil into which she has been thrown that she sinks into Eucharis' arms at the end of Act IV. However, when the two fugitives are brought back and she is confronted with them, she is unable to take a firm attitude—not only because of her exhaustion, but also because by now she has begun to be conscious of having behaved wrongly to Phaon. It is surely for this reason that she cries (when the couple are announced) "Wer rettet mich vor seinem Anblick?" (l. 1592) and averts her eyes (l. 1703) when he tells her she is unworthy of her art. Admittedly, she never expressly says she has done wrong to Phaon; but it is difficult to explain these words and gestures without assuming consciousness of guilt as their basis.

As for Phaon, his attitude to her here, in the first half of Act V, scene 3, is as negative as it was at the end of Act III (the dagger scene). There he said:

> Und wenn mir je ein Bild verflossner Tage
> In süßer Wehmut vor die Seele tritt,
> Soll schnell ein Blick auf diesen Stahl mich heilen!

And here:

> Wie anders malt' ich mir, ich blöder Tor
> Einst Sapphon aus, in frühern, schönern Tagen! (ll. 1695–6)

His attitude is intelligible enough. As Grillparzer himself said, Sappho's jealous behaviour "macht ihn durch die bei Menschen so gewöhnliche Verwechslung glauben, weil er Sapphon Unrecht thun sieht, sie sey von jeher gegen ihn im Unrecht gewesen" (III, 1, 100). Yet immediately after this, he appeals to her better nature, saying that as an artist she is only soiling herself by contact with mere humans:

> Mit Höhern, Sappho, halte du Gemeinschaft,
> Man steigt nicht ungestraft vom Göttermahle
> Herunter in den Kreis der Sterblichen.
> Der Arm, in dem die goldne Leier ruhte,
> Er ist geweiht, er fasse Niedres nicht! (ll. 1726–30)

O. E. Lessing has found this a very ill-motivated change of attitude and has said that "das ganze Intrigenspiel war offenbar nicht geeignet, jene Erkenntnis [that Sappho is semi-divine] in

Phaon wachzurufen".[26, pp. 19–20] But this verdict seems unneces-
sarily harsh. Phaon has repeatedly regarded Sappho as great and
god-like. This is how he thought of her before they ever met
(ll. 162–201), and this was still his attitude at the beginning of the
play, where his own feeling of insignificance is brought out not
only by his words of deference, but also (in Grillparzer's usual
way) by the visible contrast between "Sappho, köstlich gekleidet"
and Phaon, "ihr zur Seite in einfacher Kleidung" (directions for
their entry in I, 2). In the present context he is replying to Sappho's
charge that his love for her was a sham (l. 1723). He explains that
he loved her genuinely, but as something divine, and that only
when he met Melitta did he learn to distinguish these feelings from
warm human love. As he himself says, these reflections have
brought him to his senses (ll. 1740–1), and so instead of continuing
to abuse Sappho as a "gifterfüllte Schlange" who ought to destroy
her lyre because she is unworthy of it (ll. 1685–7), he begs her not
to desecrate the sacred arm in which she holds the instrument, as
she would do if she turned to earthly love.

Although, as we saw, she had herself, on a previous occasion,
argued that she has kinship with the gods rather than with men,
here she expressly rejects Phaon's argument, saying in an aside
that to renounce love is too high a price to pay for greatness as
an artist (ll. 1731–2). However, Phaon reiterates his point at the
end of this scene (V, 3):

> Den Menschen Liebe und den Göttern Ehrfurcht,
> Gib uns, was unser, und nimm hin, was dein!
> Bedenke, was du tust, und wer du bist!

All these words bring home to her that her violent and unreasonable behaviour is not what one is entitled to expect of someone of
her exalted calling. We saw already that her inability to look
Phaon in the face, and also the way she listens silently to his long
indictment of her, imply that she is conscious of having done
wrong. And after these final words of Phaon, the stage directions
indicate that she retires in confusion. When she returns she appears
to have taken these words to heart and to agree that her place is
among the gods, not with man.

During her absence from the stage, Rhamnes lauds her character. In Act IV she has behaved in a thoroughly unworthy manner, and Grillparzer realized that it would be necessary to restore the audience's sympathy for her. So he makes Rhamnes bring out her sterling qualities in nearly a hundred lines of verse (ll. 1812–92). We can see now one of the reasons why Grillparzer did not take Müllner's advice and delete the first Act of the play, in which (as Müllner complained) there is little action. Grillparzer replied that it was "durchaus notwending, sie noch vor dem Sturm der Leidenschaften so zu zeigen, wie sie in ihrem gewöhnlichen Zustande war, damit der Zuschauer die Arme bemitleide, statt sie zu verabscheuen". If Act I were cut, we should see little but the unpleasant side of her character, and Rhamnes' account of her exalted nature would then strike us as very unconvincing. Even as it now stands, some critics have found it not altogether easy to accept, particularly as it is made to throw Phaon and Melitta into such confusion. O. E. Lessing, for instance, notes that Phaon does not deserve the curses that Rhamnes pours upon him; that if he has behaved badly to Sappho, so has she to him, and that one would expect him to answer Rhamnes by pointing this out. Lessing believes that it is only because Grillparzer's purpose is to elevate her into an august figure that Phaon (implausibly) makes no effective reply and is made to regard himself as small beside the great Sappho. But we have already seen that, a little earlier, he had reverted to his initial elevated view of her, and it is really not at all implausible that he should accept this view now, when Rhamnes presses it upon him so forcibly.

Eucharis next reports that Sappho has assumed a statuesque appearance—"im Kreis von Marmorbildern, fast als ihresgleichen" (l. 1907); that she has taken up her lyre, donned her laurel wreath and purple robe, and looks completely transfigured:

> Wer sie jetzt sah, zum erstenmale sah, . . .
> Als Überird'sche hätt' er sie begrüßt.

There is a close correspondence between this description and the one that Phaon gives of her in Act I, when he tells how sublime she appeared when he first saw her (ll. 222–35). The earlier description prepares us for the later, and this also helps us to understand why Grillparzer declined to cut the first Act.

After Eucharis' long description, Sappho herself appears in this full regalia and announces that she has discovered her true being. In the ensuing monologue she thanks the gods for their many gifts to her. They have given her poetic capacity, fame, and even a taste of the joys of life. She argues that she has completed the task assigned to her in this world (written poetry which will bring her immortal fame), and asks them on that account not to refuse her "den letzten Lohn", that is, to remove her from this life. There is no suggestion that she feels any guilt. She does not, for instance, argue that she has sinned against the gods by wishing to renounce her art in favour of married life, and should therefore be punished by them with death.* She is asking them not for punishment but for further "Lohn" in addition to blessings already bestowed. This reward is to consist in allowing her to die before she becomes old and is mocked by fools who deem themselves wise, and by the enemies of the gods. She certainly stresses that she belongs to the gods (l. 2004), and that it would be inappropriate for anything divine to suffer weakness and sickness. When she cries to them:

> Erspart mir dieses Ringens blut'ge Qual.
> Zu schwach fühl' ich mich, länger noch zu kämpfen

she does not expressly say against whom this struggle would have to be fought, were her life to continue. The idea seems to be that she would have to fight it against her own passionate nature; for immediately afterwards she repeats (l. 2025) what Phaon had said to her "Den Menschen Liebe und den Göttern Ehrfurcht!" and she must surely have in mind the context in which this was said, namely Phaon's rebuke of her uncontrolled behaviour—a rebuke which included the injunction: "Bedenke, was du tust und wer du bist!"

In her final monologue she never once expresses her feelings of guilt towards Phaon and Melitta. It is clear enough from her

---

*Yates,[55, p. 53] however, thinks that this is her motive for suicide. But the passage he quotes in support (ll. 1995–8) does not imply that she has wronged the gods.

behaviour earlier in Act V that she has such feelings, and I think Grillparzer's reason for not making her allude to them here in the monologue which motivates her suicide was that he wished to avoid any suggestion that she dies in order to atone for her behaviour towards the couple. They are too insignificant to be the cause of her death, and so she is made to tell Phaon that he could never understand her and that they must go their separate ways (l. 1962). Phaon and Melitta are not the real causes of her death, but through them she has become aware that she can no longer be certain that she will always be able to control her passionate nature, and that she would be a very unworthy ambassador of the gods if she went on living. Her recent experiences, which we have witnessed in the play, are certainly such as to provide a genuine basis for such fears. This interpretation of her final state of mind seems to me to be more in harmony with her last words than the view that she regards her death as a punishment for betraying her art, or as a relief from unrequited love.*

Sappho is the first of Grillparzer's plays with a final Act in which the principal character adopts a new, unexpectedly calm attitude. In Sappho's case this is not exactly the dispassionate review of previous aberrations that it is with Medea, with Ottokar, and with the king in *Die Jüdin* (see below, pp. 158–9). Sappho's final criticism of her own behaviour is implicit, not directly stated; and she is really more concerned with the transgressions she would commit in the future, if she were to live on, than with her past.

As Grillparzer's second published play, *Sappho*, is a notable improvement on *Die Ahnfrau* in that it has none of the artificial

*Ehrhard's discussion of the play illustrates how perplexing critics have found its ending. He declares that her suicide would be intelligible enough if it resulted from her disappointment in love, but that such a motive is nowhere suggested in her final speech, where (he alleges) she poses as a higher being who must die as a punishment for having sullied herself with what is lowly. This he finds absurd, and asks how the poet can write about love, despair, and other emotions, if he is a superior being who must never experience them. He concludes that we can only accept Sappho's suicide if we suppose that, in spite of her apparent calm, her grief at Phaon's betrayal makes continuation of life impossible for her.(11, pp. 259–60)

motivation that disfigures the earlier work. But it still has many
repetitions, neat antitheses and other features which O. E. Lessing
has said are "im Ton der Übertreibungen jugendlicher Schillerepigonen".[26, p. 12] As an example he refers to the following
passage, where Sappho can no longer doubt that Phaon is in love
with Melitta:

> Sie schwebt vor seiner schamentblößten Stirn,
> In ihre Hülle kleiden sich die Träume,
> Die schmeichelnd sich des Falschen Lager nahn.
> Sappho verschmäht, um ihrer Sklavin willen?
> Verschmähet! Wer? Beim Himmel! und von wem?
> Bin ich dieselbe Sappho denn nicht mehr,
> Die Könige zu ihren Füßen sah
> Und, spielend mit der dargebotnen Krone,
> Die Stolzen sah und hörte, und—entließ;
> Dieselbe Sappho, die ganz Griechenland
> Mit lautem Jubel als sein Kleinod grüßte?

This outburst is, however, not just empty rhetoric. Sappho is not
only jealous of Melitta but is also beginning to realize that Phaon
is something of a nonentity. This is clearly conveyed by her
question "Verschmähet! Wer? Beim Himmel! und von wem?"
and by the contrast with the royal suitors that follows. I can only
endorse the judgement of Scherer that "Leere Rhetorik, welche
aus dem Rahmen der Situation heraustritt, um einem lyrischen
Gelüste des Dichters zu fröhnen, überhaupt jene beliebten
Kraftstellen, in denen ein Poet seine Figuren als Sprachrohr für
seine eigenen Angelegenheiten mißbraucht, werden sich bei
Grillparzer kaum finden."[42, p. 218]

2. Das goldene Vließ (1821)

A trilogy is not what one would have expected from Grillparzer,
who disliked plays where understanding what is happening at one
point presupposes memory of many previous details. This
approach, he thought, was epic and suited to a reader who can
pause to correlate passages, rather than dramatic, which means

suited to the stage. Thus in his autobiography he was critical of his decision to write *Das goldene Vließ* as a trilogy:

> Das Drama ist eine Gegenwart, es muß alles was zur Handlung gehört in sich enthalten. Die Beziehung eines Teils auf den andern gibt dem Ganzen etwas Episches, wodurch es vielleicht an Großartigkeit gewinnt, aber an Wirklichkeit und Prägnanz verliert. (I, 16, 135.)

The only acceptable type of trilogy, he adds, is Aeschylus' three independent plays linked only by their common theme, where "der durchgehende Faden verknüpft, ohne zu bedingen"—in contrast to Schiller's *Wallenstein* trilogy, which is completely epic: "Das Lager ist völlig überflüssig, und die Piccolomini sind nur etwas, weil Wallensteins Tod darauf folgt." Grillparzer's trilogy lies between these two extremes. The action of each of the first two plays is complete in itself and not merely an exposition to the third. But the third is by far the most effective, for the same reason that, in Goethe's judgement, *Wallensteins Tod* is superior to *die Piccolomini*, namely (as he wrote to Schiller, 9 March 1799): "Die Welt ist gegeben in der das alles geschieht, die Gesetze sind aufgestellt nach denen man urteilt, der Strom des Interesses, der Leidenschaft, findet sein Bette schon gegraben, in dem er hinabrollen kann."

The final play is not completely independent of the others but most of the preceding action is summarized in it (e.g. Jason's long account in Act I of how he came to woo Medea). It is independent enough to be played separately, and is the only part of the trilogy still regularly performed. Its portrayal of how bright hopes can end in disillusion is (particularly in the two opening Acts) among Grillparzer's most powerful and moving essays in pessimism. By the time its action commences, all joy has long since vanished from the lives of Medea, Gora and Jason. And by the end Kreusa, the one adult character with no trace of ruthlessness, is brutally murdered, leaving her father, the king, heartbroken.

Many of the events presupposed in Euripides' *Medea* are enacted in the first two plays of Grillparzer's trilogy. This is partly because the modern dramatist could not assume that his audience was acquainted with the details of the legend. But it is partly,

as Scherer noted, "dem Geiste des modernen Dramas gemäß".
[42, p. 236] Whereas a Greek tragedy concentrates on the final
catastrophe of a series, modern tragedies begin at the beginning,
with no trace of gloom in Act I, although there are of course
exceptions. Schiller said (in a letter to Goethe of 26 April 1799)
that the historical material for his *Maria Stuart* lent itself to what
he called "the Euripidean method" of starting after a catastrophe.
And in Schiller's play, Maria has in fact been imprisoned, tried
and condemned before the curtain rises. However, it is usual
in modern drama to begin before gloom and disaster, and to
achieve this with the Medea legend Grillparzer had to write a
trilogy.

There is a third reason why he enacts the whole story and not
just the end. In barbarian Colchis, Jason found Medea radiant
and beautiful "Im Abstich ihrer nächtlichen Umgebung" (*Medea*,
l. 457). But against a Greek background she seems sombre, even
sinister. Grillparzer wished to show not merely this common source
of human unhappiness—that the girl who thrills the youth is
repulsive to the man, so that the end of the romance is anything
but romantic—but something even more general; namely that the
ambition which drives on the young brings disillusionment when it
is fulfilled. And so he wrote of his trilogy: "Das ganze ist die
große Tragödie des Lebens, daß der Mensch in seiner Jugend
sucht, was er im Alter nicht brauchen kann."* And he made Jason
come to realize the truth of this, saying:

> Ein Jüngling war ich, ein verwegner Tor:
> Der Mann verwirft was Knaben wohlgefällt.
>
> (*Medea*, ll. 1471–2)

All this can only be brought home if we actually see Jason and
Medea full of confidence and vigour, and witness their gradual
disillusionment, and this cannot be put before our eyes in a single
play.

As the curtain rises on the first play, the one-act tragedy *Der*

---

*Quoted by Backmann.[3, p. 168] Cf. I, 17, 308.

Gastfreund, the setting leaves no doubt that the scene is barbarian territory. The stage directions read:

> Kolchis. Wilde Gegend mit Felsen und Bäumen, im Hintergrunde das Meer. Am Gestade desselben ein Altar, von unbehauenen Steinen zusammengefügt, auf dem die kolossale Bildsäule eines nackten bärtigen Mannes steht, der in seiner Rechten eine Keule, um die Schultern ein Widderfell trägt.

The barbarism suggested by the unhewn stones, the colossal size of the statue, and the wild landscape, is reinforced by the sight of Medea, bow in hand, having just shot an arrow. Later this gesture is contrasted with one which represents civilization, namely playing the lyre. When at the beginning of Act II of *Medea* she tries to learn Greek manners, she handles the instrument clumsily and complains:

> Nur an den Wurfspieß ist die Hand gewöhnt
> Und an des Weidwerks ernstlich rauh Geschäft.

Grillparzer makes the whole tragedy depend on the incompatibility between barbarism and civilization. The way the Greeks mistrust all barbarians is repeatedly stressed. To Milo Medea is "eine Barbarin, und eine Zauberin dazu", and "ein furchtbar Weib mit ihren dunkeln Augen!" (*Die Argonauten,* ll. 1101–3). Even the kind and gentle Kreusa is at first ready to believe, merely on hearsay, that she is "Ein gräßlich Weib, giftmischend, vatermörd'risch" (*Medea,* l. 330). And neither Medea nor Jason will ever forget the scorn with which she was treated on her arrival in Greece (*Medea,* ll. 251–5). But in fact Medea has none of the repulsive qualities associated with the word "barbarian". She has none of her father's covetousness and treacherousness. She is pathetically moved when Kreusa, realizing the wrong she has done her, begs her forgiveness: kindness and consideration are qualities that Medea has hardly experienced before, and the way she values them brings out her basic nobility of character (*Medea,* ll. 370–6). But she can never acquire the appearance or accomplishments of a Greek, however hard she tries, and so Jason cannot rid himself of the horror he has come to feel for this alien woman. Back in Greece, her dark eyes, which Milo had found so horrible from the first, constantly put him in mind of the serpent which guarded the fleece in Colchis, and he confesses to the king: "Und nur mit Schaudern nenn' ich sie mein Weib" (*Medea*, l. 475). We can see, then, why Grillparzer maintained that his purpose was to make the first two plays of the trilogy "so barbarisch und romantisch . . . als möglich, gerade um den Unterschied zwischen Kolchis und Griechenland herauszuheben, auf den alles ankam." And again: "Ich hatte bei der . . . Vermengung des Romantischen mit dem Klassichen nicht eine läppische Nachäfferei Shakespeares . . . im Sinne, sondern die möglichste Unterscheidung von Kolchis und Griechenland, welcher Unterschied die Grundlage der Tragik in diesem Stück ausmacht" (I, 16, 136; 159). He adds that one method he adopted to bring out the contrast was the use of free verse when the action takes place in Colchis and iambics when it is in Greece, "gleichsam als verschiedene Sprachen, hier und dort".

A good example of what he means by "das Romantische" is the stage-setting of the final Act of *Die Argonauten*. Jason and Medea stand in a cave which has "in der Felsenwand des Hintergrundes ein großes verschlossenes Tor". When Jason strikes this with his sword, "die Pforten springen auf und zeigen eine innere schmälere Höhle, seltsam beleuchtet. Im Hintergrunde ein Baum, an ihm hängt hellglänzend das goldene Vließ. Um Baum und Vließ windet sich eine ungeheure Schlange, die beim Aufspringen der Pforte ihr in dem Laub verborgenes Haupt hervorstreckt und züngelnd vor sich hin blickt." The whole incident, culminating in Jason's capture of the fleece, is not only important for the action, but brings out the horror that all the Greeks feel for barbarian magic. And the serpent's eyes, as we saw, leave an indelible impression on Jason's mind, and for ever remind him that his dark-eyed wife is a barbarian.

The principal function of the first play is to establish the fleece as a symbol. Grillparzer said he intended it to be "ein sinnliches Zeichen des ungerechten Gutes, eine Art Nibelungenhort" (I, 16, 134). It seems to confer power and victory, but there is a curse on it. Phryxus steals it, Aietes murders him for it, Jason then Pelias and Medea acquire it, Kreon seeks it—and they are all ruined. Not that it has any supernatural power. As with the picture of Rahel in *Die Jüdin*, there is no magical hocus-pocus: the fleece is simply an outward and visible sign of ill-gotten gain, and shows the evil consequences of wealth so acquired. To illustrate this, Grillparzer quoted the words Octavio speaks at the end of *Die Piccolomini:*

> Das eben ist der Fluch der bösen Tat,
> Daß sie fortzeugend Böses muß gebären.*

An evil deed, then, brings misfortune, and this in turn motivates further crimes.

In the second play, *Die Argonauten*, Jason comes to Colchis to avenge Phryxus and regain the fleece—but not for the sake of justice. Like Phryxus, he is persecuted by his family, and leaves Greece because this is the only way he can achieve fame and power, for which he is glad to risk his life:

> Ruhmvoller Tod für ruhmentblößtes Leben,
> Mag's tadeln wer da will, mich lockt der Tausch! (ll. 303-4)

When he left, he was indifferent to all else. As he tells Kreusa on his return:

> Ich hatte da kein Aug für deine Tränen
> Denn nur nach Taten dürstete mein Herz.
>
> (*Medea*, ll. 867-8)

At his first meeting with Medea, he expresses in long speeches his amazement at finding such beauty in barbarian Colchis, while the turmoil she feels prevents her from uttering anything but interjections. When armed Colchians enter, led by her brother Absyrtus, she restrains them with a gesture of her arm, thus allowing Jason to escape. At the beginning of Act II, the change that has come upon her as a result of meeting him is indicated by her friendliness and warmth to Peritta, whom she had previously scornfully repudiated as a slave of passion. (This is similar to the way Grillparzer brings out the effect on Hero of the meeting

---

*Quoted from Grillparzer's manuscript by Backmann.[3, p. 176] Cf. I, 17, 196 and 301.

with Leander by her change of attitude to Ianthe.) At their second meeting she again saves his life by warning him not to drink the poisoned cup, and then in Act III he urges her to betray her own people and follow him. For nearly 200 lines he has all the coherent speeches, and she replies with interjections, silence or tears. It is not that he is deeply in love, but he wants to enjoy the consciousness of his power by compelling her to admit her feelings. When he fails, he turns away enraged, but she then turns her face to him, stretches out her arm, and cries the one word "Jason" (l. 1327). It is enough to show that she loves him. When in the final play he recalls this incident, he says: "Und nur ihr Tun, ihr Wort verriet mir nichts" (l. 463). Here, then, the strongest emotion is expressed not with declamation but, as in real life, with broken phrases, and we find the same in most of Grillparzer's plays. Ottokar, for instance, is usually voluble enough, but when he learns that Rudolf has been elected emperor, the great shock he feels is conveyed by making him falter in the instructions he had been giving with his habitual confidence. Rudolf II of *Ein Bruderzwist* says practically nothing when he is really angry in Acts I and IV, but bangs on the floor with his stick or makes some other gesture.

Jason's emotion is not nearly as strong as Medea's and, so he can speak at length while she is silent. He sees that she loves him, and the very fact that she will not admit it in so many words angers him, and (as he concedes in retrospect, *Medea*, ll. 465–7) increases his determination to press her to a declaration. His relentlessness is brought out when he cries: "Du weinst! Umsonst; ich kenne Mitleid nicht" (l. 1264). Another motive for the ruthless pressure he brings to bear on her is revealed when he says to his companions:

> Sie kennt das Vließ, den Ort, der es verbirgt
> Mit ihr vollbringen wir's und dann zu Schiff. (ll. 1393–4)

Having claimed her as his bride, he immediately says he cares for nothing but the fleece (l. 1429). In the next Act, she threatens to kill herself if he continues his quest for it, but he merely retorts:

"Beweinen kann ich dich, rückkehren nicht" (l. 1503). Her unwillingness to help him is due partly to her conviction that she can only atone for her family's treacherous acquisition of the fleece by leaving it alone; and partly to her consciousness of how much unhappiness its possession has caused. But he is set solely on fame and glory—an attitude not infrequently taken by Grillparzer's heroes. His Sappho says despairingly of the male in general:

> Nach außen geht sein rastlos wildes Streben
> Und findet er die Lieb', bückt er sich wohl,
> Das holde Blümchen von dem Grund zu lesen,
> Besieht es, freut sich sein und steckt's dann kalt
> Zu andern Siegeszeichen auf den Helm. (ll. 820–4)

This is exactly what Jason does. In retrospect he says:

> Auf Kampf gestellt rang ich mit ihr, und wie
> Ein Abenteuer trieb ich meine Liebe. (*Medea*, ll. 466–7)

The third play begins a month after Jason and Medea's arrival in Greece, following four years at sea, during which two sons have been born to them. All that has happened in this interval is communicated by two sets of narratives—Gora's at the beginning of the first Act and Jason's at the end, which acquaints us with details omitted in Gora's briefer sketch. Both speak not simply to inform the audience, but for purposes of their own. Jason is concerned to convince the king (who interrogates him curtly and with hostile aloofness) that he is innocent, and his long speeches are punctuated only by short comments or questions from Kreon. Gora tells us less because she is addressing Medea to whom the facts are already known. While Medea is anxious to bury her past for Jason's sake, Gora reminds her of what she considers to be her guilt in deserting her country and causing, even if unwittingly, the deaths of her brother and father. Gora speaks partly from resentment—she accuses Medea of having enticed her away from her native land into slavery in Greece— and partly from motives of religious hope: to her, the change for the worse in Medea's fortunes is proof "Daß Götter sind, und daß Vergeltung ist". And this means that Jason, the chief criminal, will in turn be punished (ll. 36–7). It also means that Medea must on no account attempt to put her own actions, which have had such dire consequences, out of her mind, for this would be tantamount to denying the justice of the gods. And so Gora keeps referring to what Medea is trying to put aside. Gora's preoccupation with the gods here is not a pretext for enabling her to tell us what we need to know, but is an attitude she constantly takes, and underlies the different advice she gives Medea throughout this final play.

Another important matter to which Gora alludes is that Pelias died in mysterious circumstances, "man weiß nicht wie" (l. 80). In Grillparzer's trilogy there is no proof that Medea murdered him or committed any atrocity prior to her killing of her own children; whereas Euripides' Medea murders both her brother and Pelias, and is held in dread even by her nurse. The reason why Grillparzer mitigates her guilt is obvious enough; to keep her as the half-demented barbarian of the legend would indeed have made it easy to motivate her child-murder, but she would then have forfeited the sympathy of a modern audience.

Jason is loathed and shunned on his return to Greece because of his barbarian wife, because the Greeks could believe only the worst of a barbarian and of the man who could marry her. Gora tells her:

> Ein Greuel ist die Kolcherin dem Volke.
> Ein Schrecken die Vertraute dunkler Mächte. . . .
> Sie hassen ihn um dein, um seinetwillen.

So we can see why Medea, in the opening scene, tries quite literally to bury her past by placing her magic tools in a box and interring it, saying:

> Die Zeit der Nacht, der Zauber ist vorbei
> Und was geschieht, ob Schlimmes oder Gutes,
> Es muß geschehen am offnen Strahl des Lichts.

Her magic things are associated with night because they are

instruments of death which must be banished "aus des heitern Lebens Nähe" to which she now turns (ll. 9–10). She buries them "vor Tagesanbruch" and cries: "Der Tag bricht an—mit ihm ein neues Leben!" (l. 137). As at the beginning of *Des Meeres und der Liebe Wellen*, where Hero's happiness and confidence are brought out by the brightness of the morning sunlight, the emotions of the heroine are made clear not only by her words but by the whole situation in which we see her.

Medea buries the fleece together with her magic tools, and her address to it tells us what it has come to stand for in her mind:

> Du Zeuge von der Meinen Untergang,
> Bespritzt mit meines Vaters, Bruders Blut,
> Du Denkmal von Medeens Schmach und Schuld!

It is for Jason's sake that she is putting away her past, not, as Gora supposes, in order to wipe out this consciousness of guilt. When Gora tells her to face the facts instead of burying them she counters with:

> Geschehen ist, was nie geschehen sollte,
> Und ich bewein's und bittrer, als du denkst,
> Doch soll ich drum, ich selbst, mich selbst vernichten?
> Klar sei der Mensch und einig mit der Welt! (ll. 117–20)

"Welt" here means "environment", and to be at one with her Greek surroundings she must bury her Colchian past.

This reply to Gora also makes it clear that, although she regrets what has happened, she does not regard herself as morally guilty in Gora's sense. Gora's reiterated statements of Medea's guilt serve to remind us of how much she has sacrificed to Jason, how much grief her love for him has brought to herself and others. This needs to be emphasized so that we see the powerful motive for vengeance she will have when he deserts her. Some commentators, however, have accepted Gora's statements as the view which the dramatist is urging us to take. They are anxious to stamp some of Medea's early actions as sinful, feeling that they can thereby make her final tragedy acceptable as a just punishment.* But as she herself says, she did not kill her father, nor did her brother fall "durch mich" (ll. 333–4). The crucial action from which these and other catastrophes stem is that she loved and followed Jason; and Grillparzer impresses upon us that she was driven to this by overpowering emotions, which bewildered her as much as her family, which were not under the jurisdiction of her will and therefore are not open to moral censure—quite apart from the fact that following the man one loves is not, in normal circumstances, a crime. Even Jason, ruthless opportunist that he is, can be convicted of little outright villainy. He himself gives the best statement of the nature of his guilt:

> Ich habe nichts getan was schlimm an sich,
> Doch viel gewollt, gemöcht, gewünscht, getrachtet;
> Still zugesehen, wenn es andre taten;
> Hier Übles nicht gewollt, doch zugegriffen. (ll. 765–8)

If Medea's situation in the final play were something for which we could blame her, Grillparzer would not be prompting us to pessimistic reflections, showing in accordance with his theory how the finest characters must come to grief and tragedy; he would merely be demonstrating that certain moral shortcomings are apt

---

*For instance, Stefan Hock complains, in his otherwise excellent introduction to the play, that "sie hat die Schranken überschritten, die ihrem Wesen gesetzt sind, sie ist sich nicht treu geblieben, die Barbarin hat sich dem Griechen, die Zauberin dem Menschen verbunden. Sie hat die Heimat verlassen, ihr Magdtum preisgegeben. . . ." The moral standpoint is even clearer in the criticism of Jason that follows. "Auch er überschreitet die Schranken seiner Natur; er geht in ein Land, das ihm fremd ist und bleibt, er vermischt sich mit Greulichem, das dem Menschen stets fernbleiben soll".[19, pp. 28–9] An attitude of moral condemnation towards Medea is apparently supported by a note Grillparzer made while writing the play: "Vergiß nie, daß der Grundgedanke des letzten Stückes der ist, daß Medea, nachdem sie Kolchis verlassen, tadellos seyn *will*, aber es nicht seyn kann" (I, 17, 300). But, as Backmann has observed, Grillparzer's original plan made her guilty of the murder of Pelias on her arrival in Greece, and he seems to have made this note before he abandoned this plan. Backmann also notes that Medea's estrangement from her brutal father in the first two plays places her "in jene für sie so characteristische Mittelstellung zwischen Barbarei und Hellenentum. . . . Sie wird zu gut für Kolchis und doch nicht gut genug für Griechenland, zu einer tragischen Person gleich von vornherein."[3, pp. 133–4, 167, 173]

to have painful consequences, and this, however adequate to a Gottsched, is much too trite for a Grillparzer.

Medea's nobility of character is at its clearest in this opening Act. Her calm acceptance of all the misfortune that has befallen herself and Jason is expressed by her line: "Laß uns die Götter bitten um ein einfach Herz" (l. 86). To this, Gora replies: "Ha! Und dein Gemahl?"—knowing that, whatever Medea may do, Jason is incapable of such humility. Later, when Kreusa bids him bear his lot with "Ein einfach Herz und einen stillen Sinn" (l. 829), he can only helplessly contrast the promise of his youth with the bleak grimness of his present. Such contrasts repeatedly occur in order to bring out the tragedy of lives which had begun so auspiciously. A fine example is the short monologue which Jason begins by flinging himself despairing on a bench and crying, as he beats his breast: "Zerspreng' dein Haus und mach' dir brechend Luft!" He does not lecture on despair in the abstract, but expresses his feelings by addressing the walls of Corinth, visible in the background. This town, which harboured him as a youth, seems now so inaccessible:

> Da liegen sie, die Türme von Korinth,
> Am Meeresufer üppig hingelagert,
> Die Wiege meiner goldnen Jugendzeit!
> Dieselben, von derselben Sonn' erleuchtet,
> Nur ich ein andrer, ich in mir verwandelt.
> Ihr Götter! warum war so schön mein Morgen,
> Wenn Ihr den Abend mir so schwarz bestimmt—
> O wär'es Nacht! (ll. 203–11)

Again, ideas and emotions are expressed vividly and with immediacy by being linked with something we can actually see on the stage.

Soon after this we see Jason and Medea alone for the first time in this final play, and their conversation tells us what their relationship has become. We have seen how much Medea is prepared to do for his sake. For instance, when he had complained that her red veil is Colchian rather than Greek dress, she expressed her complaisance to his will by silently handing it to Gora. (The magic veil, which, for him, represented barbarism and which he

had taken from her in Colchis when he claimed her as Greek, she
had already buried, earlier in the scene.) But the conversation she
now has with Jason shows that she fears he will repudiate her;
and the slightest thing makes her suspicious and resentful. This
resentment gradually gains the upper hand, and in Act II we see
that she knows at heart that Gora is right, that Jason has not the
strength of character to accept misfortune with quiet resignation.
She indicts his ruthless egoism, saying:

> Nur Er ist da, Er in der weiten Welt
> Und alles Andre nichts als Stoff zu Taten. . . .
> Lockt's ihn nach Ruhm, so schlägt er einen tot,
> Will er ein Weib, so holt er eine sich,
> Was auch darüber bricht, was kümmert's ihn!   (ll. 630–6)

The speech culminates in the terrible line "Ich könnt' ihn sterben
sehn und lachen drob." Aietes had foretold that Jason would
despise her "wenn gestillt die Begier" (*Die Argonauten*, ll. 1372–4).
At the beginning of the third play he is still determined to stand
by her, although she is nothing but a burden to him (ll. 552–4).
She for her part tries desperately to suppress her fierce resentment
and to do everything to please him. In Act I he had complained
of her barbarian dress. At the beginning of Act II she appears
"griechisch gekleidet" and learning the lyre. But then Kreusa
tells her the words of the prayer that, as a boy, he used to sing to
the gods:

> Wölbt meine Brust
> Daß den Männern
> Ich obsiege
> Und den zierlichen
> Mädchen auch.

Medea is naturally put in mind of his selfishness, and although she
makes a tremendous effort to forget the wrongs he has done her,
she fails and cries "Doch das vergißt sich nicht" (l. 699).

Grillparzer has produced nothing so overpoweringly pessimistic as these first two Acts of *Medea*. The spouses have come to
hate each other, although they feel they must stay together.
Kreusa, horrified at their mutual hatred, asks: "Wer sagte mir
denn, Gatten liebten sich?" (l. 721). Jason points the pessimistic

moral when he observes, not merely that their relationship has failed to stand the test of misfortune, but the more general truth that man is worsened, not purified, by hardship and deprivation:

> Es ist des Unglücks eigentlichstes Unglück,
> Daß selten drin der Mensch sich rein bewahrt. (ll. 757–8)

We are reminded of Octavio's words about "der Fluch der bösen Tat" (see above, p. 51).

Jason goes on to exchange reminiscences with Kreusa about their happy youth. When Medea enters, she tries to attract his attention to tell him that she has learned a Greek song—a good example of her determination to assume Greek manners for his sake. What follows is a fine illustration of how Grillparzer conveys the most powerful emotions by gesture rather than by word. Jason is so absorbed in his conversation with Kreusa that Medea has to say three times "Jason, ich weiß ein Lied" before she is even heard. And then it is Kreusa who notices her and brings him to let her perform the song. He is cruelly contemptuous, and says she would do better at throwing a spear or hissing at a snake. Naturally, her confidence sinks, and so she bungles the complicated and difficult task which she had only just begun to master. Then she drops the lyre and covers her eyes with her hands to express her shame and despair. Jason tells Kreusa, a decent civilized Greek, to sing the song. But when Kreusa makes to pick up the lyre, Medea fends her off with one hand and takes it herself with the other. When Jason advances on her to retrieve it, she breaks it, shows him the broken pieces, and then throws them at Kreusa's feet. Kreusa recoils in horror at this barbarous action and cries "tot", referring of course to the lyre. Medea looks round quickly and says "Wer?—Ich lebe—lebe." And the stage directions indicate an attitude of pride and defiance. "Sie steht da hoch emporgehoben vor sich hinstarrend." The incident is closed, for there follows "von außen ein Trompetenstoß", distracting attention and preparing the arrival of the herald with his sentence of banishment. Both Medea and Kreusa have said little, but their powerful emotions have been very clearly conveyed.

By this time Jason has lost all initiative. Whereas he had earlier told the king he would stand by Medea, he now acquiesces in the king's plan that she should be banished and he wed Kreusa. Kreon is acting justly, according to his lights.* The herald's evidence (ll. 960–1005) can only confirm his opinion that Jason is innocent of Pelias' murder, while giving him good grounds for thinking that the real culprit was Medea. Thus to repudiate her will not be an injustice, while to make Jason his son and heir will protect him from the sentence of banishment which has been decreed against both Jason and Medea. Medea pleads to remain, yet cannot suppress her resentment, and she expresses these conflicting emotions when she says to Jason: "Verhaßter komm! Komm mein Gemahl!" (l. 1110). It is the same alternation between hatred and dependence that Bancbanus shows towards Otto at the end of *Ein treuer Diener*, and is expressed in the same way. We shall again meet this way of expressing an alternation between contrary emotions in Act III of *Des Meeres und der Liebe Wellen*, where Hero fiercely accuses Leander of selfishly taking risks that will jeopardize her life as well as his, and then changes her tone as her love for him begins to outweigh this resentment:

> Entsetzlicher! Verruchter!
> Was kommst du her? nichts denkend als dich selbst . . .
> Und du—Entsetzlich Bild—Leander, O!

By the end of the second Act Medea's hatred has obliterated the contrary emotion that had held it in check. She tears the Greek coat that Kreusa had given her, and says to Jason:

> Sieh! Wie ich diesen Mantel durch hier reiße
> Und einen Teil an meinen Busen drücke,
> Den andern hin dir werfe vor die Füße,
> Also zerreiß' ich meine Liebe, unsern Bund. (ll. 1125–8)

Such an explanation of what a gesture represents is not infrequent. In the second play, when Jason claims Medea as his bride, he gives visible expression to this by taking her magic veil from her,

---

*In his "Vorarbeiten" Grillparzer wrote of Kreon's "strenge Gesetz- lichkeit" and "Rechtlichkeit" (I, 17, 294 and 300). Coenan, however, finds it "impossible to detect any sense of justice" in him. [8, p. 20].

stripping her of this barbaric accessory in order to make her a Greek. He says:

> Und wie ich diesen Schleier von dir reiße,
> Durchwoben mit der Unterird's chen Zeichen,
> So reiß' ich dich von allen Banden los,
> Die dich geknüpft an dieses Landes Frevel. (ll. 1402–5)

The Act finishes with Kreon's refusal of her plea at least to be allowed to take her children into banishment. Again, it is Kreon who decides what is to happen, and Jason simply follows his initiative. Only Kreusa feels misgiving at this treatment of Medea, and asks: "Ich sinne nur, ob recht ist, was wir tun."

At the beginning of Act III Gora urges her mistress to avenge herself on Jason, and reminds her that her betrayal of her family and country for this hated Greek brought her father to his grave:

> Du hast wohl gehört, dir ward wohl Kunde
> .   .   .   .   .
> Daß er den Schmerz anfassend wie ein Schwert,
> Gen sich selber wütend, den Tod sich gab.

But Medea is more concerned with keeping her children than with thoughts of revenge. Jason, we saw, weakly accepted the king's ruling that the children must stay in Corinth. But she contrives to speak to him in the absence of the king and he gives in to her to the extent of agreeing that one of the children shall be allowed to go with her. Nowhere is Jason's injustice clearer than at this interview. He cannot deny that he urged her to murder his uncle (ll. 1082–1105, 1434–41), but there is no proof that she actually did so. Yet he acquiesces in her sentence of banishment for this crime in order to be rid of her. And this is the man for whom she has given up everything! Jason is by now completely broken. He shows no joy at the prospect of marriage with Kreusa—not only when he speaks of his future to Medea, to whom he might be expected to minimize his happiness with her rival, but even in conversation with Kreon, her father (ll. 1324–42). He can only grieve at his loss of fame and power:

> Ich bin nicht der ich war, die Kraft ist mir gebrochen,
> Und in der Brust erstorben mir der Mut. (ll. 1523–4)

His feeling of impotence and inability to take effective action is brought out by his declaration, repeated at every new development, that all has been willed by the gods.

Prior to their death in Act IV the children make three appearances. In Act I they bring out the mutual hatred of Greeks and barbarians. One of the boys asks his father whether he is a Greek, saying that, according to Gora, these are "betrügerische Leut' und feig" (l. 217). Later in Act I, Jason stands with them to plead for asylum in Corinth, and they immediately win both Kreon's and Kreusa's affection. Hence Kreon's later insistence that they should remain in Corinth and not accompany their barbarian mother into banishment. He has not merely taken a fancy to the children, but feels he must not entrust them to someone who, he believes, has committed a foul murder. They are at once drawn to the gentle Kreusa and cling to her when Medea calls them (ll. 353–6). Medea truly loves them, and is not a harsh mother— she was tactful and conciliatory to them when they taunted Jason for being a Greek (ll. 218–22). But she has none of Kreusa's sweetness, and gentleness, and this has fatal consequences. From the end of Act II, where Kreon banishes her, she repeatedly says she will go if she may take her children with her. After Jason has conceded that one of the two shall accompany her, they are brought on to the stage for the third time to see which of them will choose to follow their mother. Medea's desperation leads her to speak roughly to them, and this makes them flee to Kreusa. They do not really positively reject Medea, but are frightened— both of her manner and (as they reveal in the following Act, ll. 2042–3) of another long voyage in a ship "wo es schwindlicht ist und schwül", which they know awaits them if they accompany her (l. 1653). But here in Act III they are silent, and their behaviour naturally makes Medea think that her own—all that she has left—has turned against her. This provokes her cry:

> Wer gibt mir einen Dolch?
> Einen Dolch für mich und sie!   (ll. 1697–8)

The rest of the play is not so powerfully effective. Act IV is concerned mainly with the further motivation of Medea's murder of the children, and Act V with exonerating her and ensuring that we continue to sympathize with her. As Grillparzer himself noted, this murder is the one thing that modern audiences know of Medea, and so it must form the culmination of the play. The deed is done at the end of the only long monologue of the final play (in contrast to *Sappho*, the fleece-trilogy already shows the tendency of the mature Grillparzer to restrict the length and number of the monologues). This one not only makes Medea's motives clear but also creates a sense of suspense. The catastrophe of a play entitled *Medea* cannot come as a surprise, so while we are looking onwards, to the murder, she keeps us in suspense by reviewing her past.

The weakness of Act IV is that Grillparzer does not succeed in motivating the murder very convincingly, although the effect of this failure is not as serious as one might think; for whether the children die or not makes no difference to the tragedies of the lives of Medea and Jason. Both were so full of hope and strength, but both are now so completely broken in will and embittered that any future happiness is out of the question for either of them. If we recall Grillparzer's statement that the whole trilogy shows "die große Tragödie des Lebens", then we can understand that the killing of the children is not really essential to the tragic effect.

Medea is not set on murder at the beginning of Act III. All she knows at this stage is that she will not accept banishment (ll. 1281–2). She does think of murdering them as a means of avenging herself on Jason, but Gora dismisses this suggestion, saying: "Dich selber trifft deine Rache, nicht ihn" (l. 1235). Then Gora tells how the Greek heroes who accompanied Jason to Colchis have all met an untimtely death—evidence, for her, of divine retribution. She mentions Hercules' death when he donned a poisoned coat prepared by his wife, and Medea's interest is visibly aroused. It is clear that she is now thinking of murdering Jason (as she later does Kreusa, by sending a poisoned garment), not the children. But by the end of Act III the children have, she thinks, repudiated her, and this makes her think of revenge on them. She now begins to talk of hating them, as she hates their father whom they so strongly resemble (ll. 1776–83). This hatred for them is just a moment of desperate rage; her love is far stronger, but that too impels her to kill them. She knows that if she leaves them, as she must, they will be taunted as barbarians by the children of Jason and Kreusa:

> Oder der Ingrimm, am Herzen nagend,
> Macht sie arg, sich selbst ein Greuel.   (ll. 1794–5)

She knows what it is to become "sich selbst ein Greuel", and cries:

> Ich wollt' mein Vater hätte mich getötet,
> Da ich noch klein war,
> Noch nichts, wie jetzt, geduldet,
> Noch nichts gedacht—wie jetzt.

And again:

> Man hat mich bös genannt, ich war es nicht:
> Allein ich fühle, daß man's werden kann.   (ll. 1849–50)

These lines reiterate the truth already stated by Jason that man is worsened, not purified, by oppression and misfortune. The desire to spare her children this fate alternates with the rage and resentment that her own misfortunes have made so strong in her, and which lead her to think once more of killing her children in order to take revenge on Jason who loves them (ll. 1809–14). It is already clear that she will not kill them for one single clearly stated reason, but will be impelled by a number of motives, as is so with many acts in real life.* Even the motives already discussed do not give her the strength to do the deed. "Dem alten Wollen fehlt die alte Kraft" (l. 1860). She means that without her magic

---

*Stiefel[47, p. 40] quotes Grillparzer's note of 1820: "Medeas Gefühl gegen die Kinder muß gemischt sein aus *Haß* gegen den Vater, Jason, von dem sie weiß, daß er die Kinder liebt und ihr Tod ihm schmerzlich wird; aus *Grimm* gegen die Kinder, die sie flohen und ihren Feinden den schmerzlichen Triumph über sie verschafften; aus *Liebe* gegen eben diese Kinder, die sie nicht mutterlos unter Fremden zurücklassen will; aus *Stolz*, ihre Kinder nicht in der Gewalt ihrer Feinde zu lassen" (cf. I, 17, 306). Although he did not necessarily follow this early plan rigorously, it does show that he envisaged complex motivation of Medea's deed.

implements, which she buried in Act I, she is powerless (ll. 1869–76). But she can easily recover the box in which she interred them: "Zwei Handvoll Erde weg—und es ist mein!" And that she fails to take the necessary action means that she lacks the will-power, not just the means, to kill. It is her horror of the fleece that deters her from excavating the box. Just as the dying Pelias could not look at it without seeing the man he had murdered, so Medea fears that the sight of it will torment her with her memories of how her brother and her father died as a result of her allegiance to Jason. In the upshot, she acquires the box, and with it the strength to kill, as a result of a series of coincidences and implausible acts by others. First, the king has found the buried box, and she admits it contains the fleece which he covets—not from personal greed, but as the token of Jason's greatness. He thinks (ll. 1366–8) that if Jason has this fleece which symbolizes and proves the success of his adventure, then he will necessarily recover his power and popularity. Once again, Kreon's behaviour is not rank injustice, but must look like this to Medea and further provoke her. When the box is brought, he orders her to open it, for she alone can break the magic spell that closes it. She bids him wait, and he complies, saying that she should send the fleece to Kreusa when she does eventually open the box. What basis he has for this suggestion is not clear, but it gives Medea the idea of murdering Kreusa with the lethal instruments in the box. Next, he announces that, since Medea seems calm and co-operative, he is ready to comply with Kreusa's request that she be allowed to spend an hour with her children before she departs into banishment. It is, of course, important for the plot that they should be brought into her presence, but the king's readiness to send them is hardly convincing. He has repeatedly said that he regards her as a treacherous barbarian who will stick at nothing. And he was present when she cried out for a dagger to kill them, and herself too, when they repudiated her.

But we have yet to see how she acquires the will to kill them. The king leaves in order to send them to her. She opens the box and gives Gora a vessel from it, to be handed to Kreusa as a gift.

In spite of her later disclaimer (l. 2172) Gora must realize that
this vessel is in fact lethal, for when she accidentally raises its lid,
a flame spurts out, and she cries: "Mir ahnet Entsetzliches!"
(l. 2009). Medea then covers the vessel with the fleece, and both
with a coat. We think at once of the poisoned coat which killed
Hercules, and in which she had earlier shown so much interest.
After some hesitation, Gora does Medea's will and takes all these
things to Kreusa. This is virtually an act of suicide, for she can
reasonably anticipate that her part in Kreusa's murder will be
punished by death. It is, however, not in itself implausible that
she should give up her life. She has repeatedly said that it is
meaningless; she has long since ceased to love Medea, and the
two children to whom she had clung are now to be cut off from
her. It is for a quite different reason that her meek compliance
with Medea's will is difficult to accept. At this stage of the play she
is represented as trying to restrain her mistress, and we must see
how she comes to take this attitude.

At the beginning of the final play she was openly defiant and
justified her refusal to help bury the magic implements by saying
that she is Jason's slave, not Medea's (l. 31). She had repeatedly
urged Medea to return to Colchis, and only when the Greeks
banish her from Corinth does she change her counsel and urge
her mistress to stay, thinking that it would be shameful to return,
now that the initiative for departure has come from the Greeks.
Then, at the beginning of Act IV, she again changes her advice
and suggests flight. The change strikes Medea as remarkable:

> Und was hat dich denn so weich gemacht?
> Schnaubtest erst Grimm, und nun so zagend?   (ll. 1754–5)

Gora has become "weich" because the children have repudiated
their mother, and because in this she sees divine vengeance,
punishing Medea for abandoning her country and family. For the
rest of Act IV she tries to dissuade Medea from active revenge.
Yet finally she allows herself to be bullied into bringing about
Kreusa's death. All this is only intelligible if we consider that
Kreusa's murder is essential to the action, in that it makes Medea

feel that she must kill her children (to save them from a worse fate) and so gives her the strength she hitherto lacked. She knows that the king will avenge Kreusa by torturing and killing the children as well as herself, and this forces her hand:

> Ist's nicht schon zu spät?
> Zu spät zum verzeihn?
> Hat sie nicht schon, Kreusa, das Kleid,
> Und den Becher, den flammenden Becher?
>
> .   .   .   .   .
>
> Sie kommen, sie töten mich!
> Schonen auch der Kleinen nicht.   (ll. 2141–8)

It is doubtless because the fleece-trilogy is an early work (Grillparzer's third published play) that it shows some artificiality of motivation. But the effect of making Medea's action dependent on factors external to her (on contingencies and on badly motivated acts by others) is not entirely negative. It does impair the inevitability of the death of the children, but it also mitigates her guilt. In *Des Meeres und der Liebe Wellen* the tragedy is caused almost exclusively by the characters. Once Hero and Leander have fallen in love, it does not need any chance happenings to kill them: their passion leads them straight to their deaths. But there the passion is love and, in the case of the priest (whose action in extinguishing the lamp is so decisive), duty. With Medea the passion is of a much uglier nature, and it would be intolerable if Grillparzer showed her murder of the children determined entirely or even principally by her lust for revenge. That outer circumstances have to be invoked to play a large part in the motivation of her deed helps to reconcile us with her.* This too is the function of the second scene of the fifth Act of *Medea*. Both Jason and Medea feel annihilated, all that remains for them is (as Medea urges him) "Trage ... dulde ... büße", and she appears as the more resolute of the two in this determination to atone.

---

*Backmann notes[3, p. 167] that Grillparzer was so anxious to find "äußerer Zwang für Medeas gräßliche Tat" that he planned a scene in which she is provoked by the noise of a banquet in the palace and by shouts of "Jason hoch! Jason und Kreusa!".

In the first scene of Act V Gora is made to pass judgement on Kreusa, Jason and the king, and the stress thus placed on their guilt also has the effect of diminishing Medea's. Gora is even made to exaggerate the guilt of Kreusa and the king. The latter deprived Medea of her husband and children only because the evidence against her seemed so damning, and Kreusa had acquiesced for the same reason, but even then with misgivings. It is without justification when Gora asks of her: "Warum griff sie nach des Unglücks letzter Habe?" But what really matters at this stage is not whether what they had done is just but that we should be conscious of the undeniable fact that the natural effect of their deeds was to goad Medea to desperation, as if she were a hunted beast. Gora says to the two men:

> Habt ihr es nicht umstellt mit Jägernetzen
> Des schändlichen Verrats, das edle Wild,
> Bis ohne Ausweg, in Verzweiflungswut,
> Es, überspringend euer Garn, die Krone,
> Des hohen Hauptes königlichen Schmuck,
> Mißbraucht zum Werkzeug ungewohnten Mords. (ll. 2245–50)

It is obvious that the effect is to exonerate Medea. And the final scene of the play elevates her further. It has something of the transfiguration of the heroine at the end of Euripides' play, where she appears on a chariot drawn by winged dragons, which finally rises into the air. Grillparzer gives her more than natural knowledge when he makes her tell Jason that she is not destined to fall by his hand, and that they will never again confront each other. Furthermore, her meeting with Jason here is not motivated in the ordinary sense. She seems to know where to find him.*

Grillparzer's trilogy ends with an allusion to the symbolism of the fleece. Medea is on her way to return it to the temple at Delphi. She shows it to Jason, saying:

> Erkennst das Zeichen du, um das du rangst?
> Das dir ein Ruhm war und ein Glück dir schien?
> Was ist der Erde Glück?—ein Schatten!

---

*Grillparzer noted that in her final appearance she speaks with Jason "etwa wie ein abgeschiedener Geist über das Ereignis reden könnte, etwa wie der Chor bei den Alten" (I, 17, 297).

> Was ist der Erde Ruhm?—ein Traum!
> Du Armer! Der von Schatten du geträumt!
> Der Traum ist aus, allein die Nacht noch nicht.

The parallel with what Rustan says when he awakens at the end of *Der Traum ein Leben* (see above, p. 17) is striking. As Professor Yuill has said[56, p. xxiii] Rustan gives the same message of resignation, but in a less sombre light, since his terrifying dream prevents him from embarking on the course that has led Medea and Jason to ruin.

3. Des Meeres und der Liebe Wellen (1831)

Modern writers who treat themes from classical antiquity often do so in order to write about love, and Grillparzer's plays on Greek material all depict love's first awakening in young people, although only *Des Meeres und der Liebe Wellen* is restricted to this theme. As in his two other Greek plays, the story is not about the real historical world of Athens or Sparta, but is taken from myth and legend. Free from the limitations which go with a historical setting, these plays show human emotions and problems common to all ages and special to none.

Des Meeres und der Liebe Wellen is essentially a study in a girl's growth to womanhood. All the other characters, even her partner, are less important than she. Her opening monologue, spoken on the morning of the day she is to be consecrated priestess, is a splendid piece of character-drawing. Almost her first words bring out her pride at the thought of the career which is to be initiated at the ceremony:

> Und ich bin dieses Festes Gegenstand.
> Mir wird vergönnt, die unbemerkten Tage,
> Die fernhin rollen ohne Richt und Ziel,
> Dem Dienst der hohen Himmlischen zu weihn;
> Die einzelnen, die Wiesenblümchen gleich,
> Der Fuß des Wanderers zertritt und knickt,
> Zum Kranz gewunden um der Göttin Haupt,
> Zu weihen und verklären. Sie und mich.

Like her uncle, she is proud of her descent from a family of priests (ll. 20–3) and very conscious of her superiority to "der Schwarm" —the common herd, who leave undone those things which they ought to have done (ll. 52–3), while she rectifies their omissions with complacency. Her playful mockery of Hymen, god of marriage (ll. 33–7), and of Amor, shows that she is glad to enter upon the celibate life of a priestess and does not regard it as a sacrifice. When Ianthe suggests that Hero, like any other girl, would have stolen a glance through the gate at the youths waiting to be admitted to the festival, she is visibly angered and tells Ianthe, not once but repeatedly, to silence her wanton tongue:

> Sprich nicht und reg dich nicht' (l. 85)
>
> . . . . .
>
> Du sollst nicht reden, sag' ich, nicht ein Wort! (l. 90)

And her uncle's suggestion that her mother will arrive "mit dem Bräut'gam an der Hand" (l. 216) provokes likewise a strong reaction. She accuses him of tactless and hurtful joking (l. 217) and turns her back on him—the strongest gesture she can make to one who (unlike the servant girls) is her superior.

Grillparzer makes her lack of interest in young men understandable enough. Those she has met have all been like her brother:

> Vom gleichem Sinn und störrisch wildem Wesen.
> Das ehrne Band der Roheit um die Stirn,
> Je minder denkend, um so heft'ger wollend. (ll. 308–10)

The temple, where she has spent the last eight years, has been in every respect a place of peace and refuge for her. She came to it from the rancour and discord of an unhappy home (ll. 201–4) in a society where women had duties but no rights—whereas "Im Tempel hier hat auch die Frau ein Recht" (l. 279). So for her the temple represents calm and happiness, and she is not conscious of making any sacrifice in renouncing normal life: "Hier ist kein Krieg, hier schlägt man keine Wunden" (l. 389). The sequel shows that it is otherwise.

Papst, who is well aware that Hero's experience of men and of

normal life have been distasteful to her, nevertheless supposes
that her readiness to renounce them is due to suppression of
subconscious desire for erotic experience; that her renunciation
is so emphatic as to suggest resolution of an "inner conflict" of
this kind. My view is that the motives of which Grillparzer shows
her conscious are adequate to explain her attitude. Papst also
interprets the sharpness of her replies to Ianthe's suggestions as
evidence of "subconscious fear of admitting to herself even the
possibility of their partial truth", while I think that Hero's sharp
manner testifies to her consciousness of her superiority over
ordinary girls. He also mentions her father's reference (l. 250) to
"kleinlich dunkle Zweifel", and interprets these as Hero's doubts as
to her suitability for the priesthood, these being in turn interpreted
as caused by subconscious desire for love that is incompatible with
office. But the "Zweifel" are clearly not Hero's at all, but her
mother's. The subconscious has become an unfortunate adjunct of
recent literary criticism, and Papst goes so far as to distinguish, as
a specifically Austrian element in Grillparzer's heritage, a "highly
developed sensitivity to twilight mental states on the borderland
between the conscious and the subconscious".[33, pp. 17, 29–30, 50]
I do not wish to deny that much in human thought and behaviour
is unconscious, nor that dramatists sometimes represent characters as impelled by motives of which they are not conscious. But
it seems to me that the subconscious motives that critics sometimes
discern contribute more to their own reputation for subtlety than
to the elucidation of the play. I would remind the reader of
Grillparzer's words quoted as the motto of this book.

Although, to my mind, Hero is not repressing any desires, she
certainly does not know her potentialities. Already in this first
Act Grillparzer shows that she is not really a dedicated priestess.
She is represented as finding peace and calm in the practical duties
of her office. We first see her as she decorates the temple with
flowers, and she envisages her future days:

> Einförmig still, den Wasserkrug zur Hand,
> Beschäftigt, wie bisher, an den Altären;
> Und fort so Tag um Tag.   (ll. 396–8)

She does not even understand her uncle's suggestion that she
should become a seer and commune with the goddess by night.
"Du hast mich nicht gefaßt", he says (l. 136), showing how much
more her mind is on this world than is his, even though she is less
worldly than the servant girls whom she had in turn professed,
with haughty disdain, not to understand (l. 65). When he explains
what he meant, she immediately rejects his suggestion:

> Verschiednes geben Götter an Verschiedne;
> Mich haben sie zur Seh'rin nicht bestimmt.
> Auch ist die Nacht zu ruhn; der Tag, zu wirken,
> Ich kann mich freuen nur am Strahl des Lichts.   (ll. 184–7)

How much irony there is here! She is to find in Act III that the
night is not for rest, in Act IV that in her exhaustion she cannot
"wirken" throughout the day, and that instead of rejoicing in it
she longs for night.

In these opening incidents of Act I her character is also brought
out by contrast with her parents. Her father's pride is not, like
Hero's and the priest's, centred on higher things, but is that of the
pompous petit-bourgeois, as is clear when he goes out of his way
to mention how he is envied because of

> . . . das Amt, mit dem seit manchem Jahr
> Bekleidet das Vertraun mich unsrer Stadt.   (ll. 238–9)

Only with reluctance does he leave his wife and daughter to speak
alone, since he knows that his wife would gladly persuade Hero
to return home instead of becoming a priestess and filling his
heart with pride. The mother is too upset to say much, and while
Hero talks to her in the front of the stage, a dove which had made
its nest in a bush at the back is removed by the Tempelhüter, with
Hero's uncle and father watching. This brings some action into a
scene which is otherwise limited to character-drawing, and this
action is in turn made to effect a further portrayal of character,
for the mother sees her own fate reflected in the treatment of the
dove:

> Unschuldig fromme Vögel stören sie
> Und nehmen aus ihr Nest. So reißen sie
> Das Kind auch von der Mutter, Herz vom Herzen.   (ll. 338–40)

Furthermore, just before this, Hero has said that she proposes

> Hier an der Göttin Altar, meiner Frau,
> Das Rechte tun, nicht weil man mirs befahl,
> Nein, weil es recht, weil ich es so erkannt. (ll. 333-5)

There could be no clearer illustration of her independence than the way she goes on to ignore the temple rule that "All was sich paart bleibt ferne diesem Hause" (l. 357), and to caress the dove which the others had been trying to remove. Scherer rightly stresses her independence as an important factor in motivating her death. "Sie hält von ihrem Wesen jegliche Störung fern. Sie will den eigenen Sinn bewahren, ablehnend alles Übrige.... Solche Unabhängigkeit kann sich nicht leidend fügen und nach thränenreichen Klagen ins Unvermeidliche schicken. Wenn sie das Unglück trifft, zerbricht sie".(42, pp. 258-9)

When Hero leaves the stage to dress for the ceremony, the crowd of spectators gathers. It includes Naukleros, who is talkative and cheeky, and Leander, who says not a single word in this first Act. He is still suffering from what Naukleros calls "der alte Trübsinn", brought on by his mother's death. But although he does not speak in Act I, he does (urged on by Naukleros) raise his eyes from the ground at the point in the ceremony when Hero stands in front of him and speaks the formula to renounce Hymen. As their eyes meet, she is overcome with confusion, expressed by her hesitation, which she excuses by saying that she has forgotten the tongs for putting incense on the altar fire—only to be told that she is holding them in her hand! When she begins to speak the formula, it is the wrong one, and she then clumsily puts too much incense on, making the flame surge up. It is quite natural that Leander should attract her, for he is a peaceable fellow, has been a good son to his mother, and his friend calls him "dumpfer Träumer, blöder Schlucker". Although these details are given only later, she must see from his whole appearance that he is quite unlike what she has hitherto understood a man to be. In *Das goldene Vließ* Medea's irresistible attraction to Jason is something we must accept as a datum. That in *Des Meeres und der Liebe*

Wellen Grillparzer gives such clear indications of what basis Hero has for her love for Leander shows how much more the emphasis is on love here.

Act II draws Leander's character as Act I has done Hero's. He still says little, and Naukleros does nearly all the talking. He is used to Leander's gloomy silence, but learns now of its new cause. Leander's despair is expressed in the one terse line: "Ich wußt' es ja. Komm Nacht! Und so ists aus" (l. 677). When Hero enters, on her way to draw water, her song of Leda and the swan (to which she repeatedly returns even though her uncle has forbidden it to her) shows that she is not now quite uninterested in love. That such a song should rise to her lips at this juncture is as significant as Gretchen's singing of "Der König in Thule" just after the first encounter with the handsome young stranger. Leander is too shy to approach her (a touch very true to his character) and he has to be taunted by the forward and cheeky Naukleros before he can bring himself to rush forward and fling himself at her feet. Naukleros tells her, in his usual forthright manner, that her eyes have made Leander a sick man, and she reacts sharply—as she had twice done in Act I—to suggestions that she is capable of love:

> frech ist der Menge Sinn,
> Und ehrfurchtslos, und ohne Scheu und Sitte.

But when Leander raises his head and she sees that he is the youth whose eyes she had caught at the festival, she changes her tone and addresses him as "guter Jüngling". There is no further trace of anger, and at this stage she feels, if not love, then at least compassion, calling him "armer Mann" and saying: "Er ist so schön, so jugendlich, so gut." When her uncle arrives, she does not hesitate to deceive him in order to explain why she is in conversation with the two youths. He urges them to leave at once, for they have no right to stay after midday:

> Denn wenn die Sonn auf ihres Wandels Zinne
> Mit durst'gen Zügen auf die Schatten trinkt,
> Dann tönen her vom Tempel krumme Hörner
> Dem Feste Schluß, dir kündigend Gefahr. (ll. 836–9)

The use of this striking image to state the shortening of shadows at midday is a good example of Grillparzer's manner of conveying ordinary facts.*

At the beginning of Act III we see how greatly Hero's mind is pre-occupied with Leander. She is unresponsive to her uncle's long speeches as he introduces her to the tower where she is to live as priestess. He is hurt by her obvious indifference to what moves him so deeply, and warns her not to be unfaithful to her charge:

> Du fändest auch in mir den Mann, der willig,
> Das eigne Blut aus diesen Adern gösse,
> Wüßte er nur einen Tropfen in der Mischung,
> Der Unrecht birgt, und Unerlaubtes hegt.

Both Hero and Leander have been, and are to be, warned repeatedly that to indulge their passion will be dangerous to themselves and others. The priest's remark in Act I about a bridegroom for her was not the tactless joking for which she took it, but a determination on his part to make quite sure that she is suited for the celibate life. Just before the consecration ceremony he said: "Wüßt' ich sie schwach, noch jetzt entließ' ich sie" (l. 407). Here, in Act III, he is at first reassured when she answers his reproach with an assurance that "Sammlung wird mir werden, glaube mir". He becomes ecstatic at the thought of the efficacy of "Sammlung"—but when she declares that such flights are beyond her he finds her pedestrian attitude to her exalted vocation "ärmlich", and his memory of the incident in the grove with the two youths makes him go on to warn her, saying "Den ersten Anlaß meid!" When he has left, she voices her awareness that this single day has changed her more than whole years have done, and that whole years will not suffice to obliterate it:

> Wie vieles lehrt ein Tag, und ach, wie wenig
> Gibt und vergißt ein Jahr.—Nun er ist fern.

When shortly afterwards Leander enters her room, she indeed again calls him "guter Jüngling", but firmly bids him go. At this

---

*Cf. below, p. 143, for other examples and comment on Grillparzer's method.

stage she still feels first and foremost a priestess, and tells him how her people treat a priestess who has a lover:

> Mein Volk . . .
> Es schonet zwar das Leben der Verirrten
> Allein stößt aus sie, und verachtet sie,
> Zugleich ihr ganzes Haus und all die Ihren.

It is thus clear that her later surrender is not due to ignorance of what is at stake. Nor do these words imply that she wishes to continue to see Leander but is afraid of the consequences, for she gives the information only in reply to his inquiry about the fate of an erring priestess, and makes it quite clear that the principal reason for her rejection of him is "weil ich nur schwach erwidre deine Meinung". Grillparzer himself noted that "nie soll Hero darauf ein besonderes Gewicht legen, daß jenes Verhältnis verbothen, oder vielmehr strafbar sey. Es ist mehr ihr Inneres, das sich früher nicht zur Liebe hinneigte, und das nicht ohne Widerstreben nachgibt, als daß sie ein Äußeres fürchtete" (I, 19, 232). Thus in Act I she renounced love because she had never known it. When she comes to know it she at first resists it: she tries to dissuade Leander both in Act II, in the grove, and here in Act III, in the tower. But these new feelings she finds so disturbing rapidly come to dominate her, and the very title of the play alludes to the change which is wrought in her. Up to Act III the sea is calm:

> Der Hellespont
> Läßt Kindern gleich die frommen Wellen spielen;
> Sie flüstern kaum, so still sind sie vergnügt   (ll. 1027–9)

But the rise of a strong wind can completely transform it, as Hero's initial calm contentment with the religious life is transformed by her encounter with Leander. Both the waves of the sea and those of love can arise suddenly with destructive force to which all else must yield.

The fourth Act is the longest of all, yet contains little outer action. Hero is shown as thinking only of her love, and makes no attempt to hide evidence that incriminates her—her fatigue after the sleepless night, her change of attitude to Ianthe. She is needlessly tactless to the Tempelhüter, and actually provokes him into seeking evidence of her guilt. And he in turn influences the priest, who throughout the Act gropes his way towards the conclusion that she is guilty. Grillparzer noted, in continuation of the passage last quoted, that "Im IV Akte ist ... keine Spur von Ängstlichkeit in Heros Wesen, obschon es ihr ziemlich nahe liegt daß man Verdacht geschöpft habe. Sie ist schon wieder ins Gleichgewicht des Gefühls gekommen, aber eines neuen, des Gefühls als Weib." Once again we see how independent she is. To decide what is right or wrong she follows not convention nor authority, but her own feelings. In Act IV she defines duty as:

> das alles, was ein ruhig Herz,
> Im Einklang mit sich selbst und mit der Welt,
> Dem Recht genüber stellt der andern Menschen. (ll. 1732–4)

Her view of her rights and duties changes because her feelings, on which this view is based, change so drastically in the course of the play.

The priest has three important monologues in this fourth Act. They serve to show how he is gradually convinced by the mounting evidence of Hero's guilt, and also to underline that it is as custodian of the divine law that he acts to thwart the lovers. Thus he says: "In meinem Innern reget sich ein Gott" (l. 1365) and he addresses Leander in his thoughts:

> Unseliger, was strecktest du die Hand
> Nach meinem Kind, nach meiner Götter Eigen? (ll. 1517–18)

Unfortunately his behaviour in Act V suggests that his motives are not as pure and disinterested as he wishes to represent them. When Leander's body is discovered, he lies to Ianthe about Hero's relation to the youth (ll. 1910–13), even though he had earlier said

> Der Tücht'ge sieht in jedem Soll ein Muß
> Und Zwang, als erste Pflicht, ist ihm die Wahrheit.
>
> (ll. 415–16)

And he resorts to mean threats in order to ensure that the whole matter will be hushed up. It is difficult to avoid the inference that he fears Hero's transgression will be punished upon her whole family, as she herself had said would be the case. The scorn with which Ianthe treats him at the end is a just indictment of the way his concern with his own status has led him to drive Hero to her death. It is only in Act V that his behaviour appears in any way selfish, and the obtrusion of such motives comes as something of a shock after his apparent disinterestedness. It was doubtless with Act V in mind that Grillparzer said "die Figur des Priesters ist zu kurz gekommen" (II, 10, 178).

In his third monologue in Act IV he makes a final attempt to convince himself of Hero's innocence, but she herself provides the evidence of her guilt by lighting the lamp which is to guide Leander to her tower. When she falls asleep, exhausted after the day which the priest has deliberately made as tiring as possible for her, he turns to the lamp and cries: "Der Götter Sturm verlösche deine Flamme." The Tempelhüter's monologue expresses the suspense we all feel at this crucial point in the action. He asks, as the priest is about to extinguish the lamp: "Was sinnt er nur? Mir wird so bang und schwer." In Grillparzer's sources it was put out by a storm, but he changed this contingency into an action motivated primarily by impersonal devotion to religious principles. The priest's purity of motive is suggested by contrast with the Tempelhüter, who has been stung by Hero's taunts into making a damning case against her. Now that he has done so, he begins to pity her:

> —Unselig Mädchen!
> Erwacht sie? Nein. So warnet dich kein Traum?
> Mich schaudert. Weh! Hätt' ich mein Oberkleid!

Unlike the priest, who is an educated man with his principles very much in mind, the Tempelhüter is an unsophisticated person whose actions are prompted directly by his feelings—first resentment and here sympathy. To use the monologue to voice such fears and misgivings at a crucial moment is a common dramatic device. We have only to think of Leicester's monologue as Maria Stuart is executed, or of Mirza's while Judith and Holofernes are together in the tent.*

*Schiller, *Maria Stuart*, Act V, scene 10; Hebbel, *Judith*, Act V.

Act IV consists of three scenes, and the central one takes us back to Naukleros and Leander, who are now in Abydos. This scene fills out the time interval between the first, which takes place after Leander's departure from Sestos in the morning, and the last of the Act, in which Hero falls asleep as she waits for him to return in the evening. It also shows the marked change that has come over him in consequence of the vitalizing experience of love. It is the last time we are to see him alive, and the words of the priest at the end of the previous scene as he lays the snare make us very conscious of the peril that awaits him. It is tragically ironical that he has now lost all traces of his former melancholy. His defiance of Naukleros, who tries to restrain him, forms one of the few rhetorical, declamatory outbursts in the play:

> Tor, der du bist! und denkst du den zu halten,
> Den alle Götter schützen, leitet ihre Macht?
> Was mir bestimmt, ich wills, ich werds erfüllen:
> Kein Sterblicher hält Götterwalten auf.

His prayer to the gods is in the same style:

> Poseidon, mächt'ger Gott!
> Der du die Wasser legtest an die Zügel,
> Den Tod mir scheuchtest von dem feuchten Mund.
> Zeus, mächtig über Allen, hehr und groß!
> Und Liebesgöttin, du, die mich berief,
> Den kundlos Neuen, lernend zu belehren
> Die Unberichteten was dein Gebot.
> Steht ihr mir bei und leitet wie bisher!

Comparable passages are spoken by Hero in Act V when she turns on her uncle and curses him loudly, instead of concealing what has happened, and then bids the dead Leander farewell. Such declamation is the more effective because restricted to points of powerful emotion, and also because the zest of the lover, the indignation of the wronged and the grief of the bereaved are of general interest. Tragedy commonly includes speeches which, even in isolation from their context, appeal because they express ideas and emotions of general interest. For maximum effectiveness each speech must be relevant to the situation in which it is made (as Grillparzer himself insisted, see above, p. 14) and not form an unrelated strand. But if it is of no interest in itself, but only a means of reaching a final tragic situation, we might well be bored before the end. Grillparzer makes both these points by implication when he says: "Das ist der innere Zusammenhang des Drama, daß jede Szene ein Bedürfnis erregen, und jede eines befriedigen muß" (II, 11, 75). And the latter end can be achieved if the scene includes passages which are relevant to a wider context than their immediate one. The following extract from Hero's farewell to Leander, for instance, expresses not merely her personal emotion, but the bewilderment universally felt at the sudden loss of one to whom one is conscious of owing much:

> Nie wieder dich zu sehn, im Leben nie!
> Der du einhergingst im Gewand der Nacht
> Und Licht mir strahltest in die dunkle Seele,
> Aufblühen machtest all, was hold und gut,
> Du fort von hier an einsam dunkeln Ort,
> Und nimmer sieht mein lechzend Aug' dich wieder?
> Der Tag wird kommen und die stille Nacht,
> Der Lenz, der Herbst, des langen Sommers Freuden,
> Du aber nie, Leander, hörst du? nie!
> Nie, nimmer, nimmer, nie!

When I speak of the "rhetoric" of this and other speeches in the play, I have in mind features of style and diction that are often present when a speaker expresses emotion to an audience. In real life a sincere public speaker may use expressions which would not be used in conversation, and he may employ figures of speech, repetitions, inversions, enumerations and other peculiarities as the spontaneous result of his emotional delivery. A speaker may also employ them to simulate an emotion, and in either case we may call his style "rhetorical". Now the dramatic character is a creation of the dramatist, and so his words will not normally be the spontaneous effect of emotion. We cannot suppose that Grillparzer, writing Hero's farewell to Leander, felt the full strength of emotion he represents her as feeling. Nevertheless, what she is made to say is effective because the emotion she expresses is one with which we are familiar, and in which we are ready to participate, and also because the whole play has built up this situation in which a strong expression of this emotion is appropriate. If either circumstance were altered—if the emotion were unfamiliar or appeared uncalled for—we should be conscious of the artificiality of what she says, and this would destroy all appearance of sincerity. Even when the emotion is familiar and appropriate the effect may be destroyed if the style is recognizably derived from some literary model or if a particular trick is repeated so often that we become aware of it. I indicated above (pp. 2–4) that this is sometimes the case (or has often been regarded as so, fc. p. 46) in Grillparzer's earliest plays.

Hero's death when the priest tears her from Leander's body is intelligible not only from her independence (the factor stressed by Scherer) but also from the swiftness with which one drastic change in her life has followed another. Grillparzer noted in his autobiography that one reason for concentrating the events of a play into a short period is that "die Zeit ist nicht nur die äußere Form der Handlung: sie gehört auch unter die Motive: Empfindungen und Leidenschaften werden stärker oder schwächer durch die Zeit" (I, 16, 168). What he surely had in mind is that when events follow each other quickly the characters are forced into reactions they would not have chosen had the pace been more leisurely. In this play, Hero is unable to adjust herself to her sudden bereavement which follows so hard upon an equally drastic change from priestess to lover.

Of all Grillparzer's plays this one has perhaps suffered most from the "close analysis" that informs so much recent literary criticism. Miss Atkinson's discussion of it[1, pp. 261 ff.] is a good example. In Act I Hero is seen against a background of sunlight, is said to tread a radiant path in casting aside earthly ties to become a priestess, and can find no pleasure in nocturnal vigils. Miss Atkinson infers that these details link her with sunlight so closely that later references to it may plausibly be interpreted as meaning her! Leander, on the other hand, "is immediately identified with darkness", for he is dark-skinned and depressed, and so references to shadows are likely to be really references to him. It is from these premises that Miss Atkinson comments on the four lines in which the priest explains to Naukleros and Leander that they must depart by midday (see above, p. 74), and she argues that his image of the sun drinking the shadows is "a hint that Hero's love has the power to disperse the shadows that beset Leander" (i.e. his depression). Miss Atkinson has herself shown very clearly that some of the references to light in Act I bring out the cheerfulness, happiness and confidence the heroine feels at this stage, and that many later references to light and darkness are natural enough in a play in which lovers are prevented by guards from meeting except at night, and the catastrophe is brought about by the extinction of a light. It seems, then, unnecessary to assume the complicated symbolism that she invokes on such a flimsy basis.

Papst's interpretation of the play is likewise in part spoiled by this quest for symbols. He also will correlate two words or incidents which have some similarity (however trivial) and assign a like symbolic meaning to both. At the end of Act IV Hero loosens her shoe as she assumes a reclining posture and thereby indicates that she will not be able to remain awake for long. Papst links this with the end of Act I where, he says, "Hero, hurried off by the Priest, fumbles at her shoe, while her eyes glance over her right shoulder and alight once more on Leander".[33, p. 27] His argument is that in both cases her behaviour to the shoe symbolizes "a relaxation of her powers of conscious control". But in actual fact she does not "fumble at" her shoe in Act I, but merely looks over her shoulder at Leander as if she were looking at some defect in her shoe that had drawn her attention. It is difficult to avoid the conclusion that Papst has made the shoe more prominent in this incident and has made her at least touch, if not loosen it, in order to link this with the later loosening and so facilitate a common symbolic interpretation of both.

CHAPTER 3

THE HISTORICAL DRAMAS

1. König Ottokars Glück und Ende (1825)

Grillparzer's plays on Greek legends are love plays in which the main action consists of few episodes and the unities of time and place are, more or less, kept. To concentrate the career of a historical personage into a unified series of events calls for much greater skill. If the dramatist is to show not merely his hero's fall, but all the conditions which lead to it, then the action must span a considerable period, and incidents which occurred in many different places must be brought together. Furthermore, instead of two lovers, a large number of personages will be involved. In *König Ottokar*, written in 1823 and first performed two years later, Grillparzer portrays the career of Bohemia's greatest king, Premysl Ottokar II. His refusal to accept the sovereignty of Germany in 1256 marked the beginning of the Great Interregnum, which was terminated only by the election of Rudolf of Habsburg as Emperor in 1273. Ottokar's policy was to keep the Empire weak while expanding his own kingdom. He gained territory by marriage with Margaret of Austria, nearly twenty years his senior, whom he repudiated before her death in 1267 in favour of a Hungarian princess. Bela IV of Hungary attempted to recover Styria from him, but Ottokar defeated him in 1260, and in 1269 he inherited Carinthia and Carniola. When Rudolf became Emperor he was determined to wrest the fiefs of Austria, Styria, Carinthia and Carniola from Ottokar, and for this purpose he made an alliance with the Pope (1275) and then summoned Ottokar to the diet to justify his occupation of them. When

Ottokar refused to attend, Rudolf led an army into Austria and defeated him in 1276. The struggle was renewed two years later, by which time it was Ottokar who had obtained Papal (and other) support. But he had failed to conciliate the nobles of Austria and Styria, and Hungary also opposed him. So also did many of his own Bohemians since he had done so much to encourage German settlers in his lands. He was defeated and killed in battle in 1278.

The action of Grillparzer's play extends from Ottokar's victory over the Hungarians in 1260 to his death in 1278, and the events are concentrated into two years (as we can infer from l. 2561). In the first Act events spread over many years are put into a single day. They include Ottokar's return from his victory at Marchegg, the departure of Margareta and the arrival of Kunigunde, the offer of the imperial crown, the homage of the Styrians, the expulsion of the Bohemians from the suburbs of Prague to make room for German craftsmen, and the death of Ulrich, Duke of Carinthia.* Grillparzer introduces Ottokar when, at the height of his power and fame after his victory, he has decided to repudiate Margareta. A particularly effective result of the concentration of events is that the new wife appears on the stage before the old one has left it, whereas in history Kunigunde arrived months after Margareta's departure. Everything prior to the repudiation of Margareta is narrated, e.g. the unrest in Austria which led her to marry Ottokar, and his victory at Marchegg. As usual with Grillparzer, the facts are stated by characters who have a plausible reason for giving them, independent of the dramatist's need to inform us. Thus the victory is narrated by Zawisch (one of Grillparzer's few villains) to Benesch and Milota, although they already know of it and are anxious instead for news about whom the king is to marry after his divorce. Zawisch tells them what they already know in order to increase their impatience. Such behaviour is quite in accord with his cynical mockery, and there is none of the loss of plausibility that normally occurs when one

---

*Klaar dates the expulsion of the Bohemians as early as 1254 and the offer of the imperial crown as late as 1271, although he mentions authorities which place this latter event in 1256. See ref. 22, pp. 21, 48–9.

character tells another what is already known to both. We may compare the motivation here with the way in which Leon tells all and sundry of his intentions. This would normally be a feeble way of conveying character and plans, but in this particular case is quite plausible, since Leon has accepted an obligation to tell the truth.

Ottokar's repudiation of Margareta is the central episode in this first Act, and its consequences fill the remaining ones. Having gained Austria by marriage with her he now seeks more territory from another marriage. It is this deed that leads to all the opposition against him, and in particular brings him into conflict with Rudolf, who has hitherto been his friend and voluntarily fought in his battles. Grillparzer has deviated from the facts here, for in reality the conflict between the two men developed years after Ottokar's divorce, at a time when Ottokar was challenging Rudolf's authority as Emperor by failing to attend the diet to which he had been summoned. Grillparzer has placed the seeds of the conflict in the moral—not the political—differences between them, and so has initiated it before, not after, Rudolf's election. Again, in the sources, the defection of the Austrian and Styrian nobles occurs as a result of many isolated acts of tyranny by Ottokar. Grillparzer has achieved greater clarity by making their defection a direct result of the repudiation of Margareta, the central fact of the play, and one that is not merely narrated, for the final legal proceedings which dissolve the marriage take place on the stage.

One is in particular struck by the continuity of this first Act. In both its two scenes each incident leads naturally into the next. At the beginning the atmosphere of alarm and worry about the queen is set by agitated behaviour and by the broken dialogue. In the conversation that follows between Merenberg and his son Seyfried, broken lines again express strong emotion—Seyfried's anger—and the instructions he receives to complain to the "Reich" at Frankfurt about Ottokar's treatment of Margareta, constitute the first indication that the king is alienating the Styrian nobles by his treatment of this Austrian princess.

In the ensuing conversation between Seyfried and the Rosenbergs, Grillparzer's skill in individual characterization appears when each of the Rosenbergs reacts differently to the news that Ottokar's new wife is to be Kunigunde, the grandchild of the King of Hungary, not their kinswoman Berta as they had been led to believe. Benesch rants and vents his impotent fury; Milota calmly and calculatedly determines on vengeance (although, as we shall see, his patriotic pride in Bohemia counteracts his hostility to the king to whom it owes its greatness); Zawisch hides his plans under a cloak of cynicism. Ottokar's loyal supporters are also strikingly differentiated. The wild-blooded Füllenstein is a very different man from the restrained and far-seeing Chancellor Braun von Olmütz.

Margareta dominates both the beginning and end of the play, but is absent from the intervening Acts; the first Act is one extended portrayal of Ottokar's injustice to her, and in Act V Grillparzer has deviated from historical facts to confront him with her dead body. Margareta, then, is another example of a character who acts as a framework to the play, like the king in *Ein treuer Diener* and the bishop in *Weh dem, der lügt!* But whereas they are introduced to set the problem which dominates the remaining action, Margareta's function is to bring out Ottokar's character—the ruthless injustice which is the cause of all the opposition that leads to his downfall, and his change of character at the end, when the king who could not even bear to witness kneeling (l. 2454) after his own kneeling had brought him shame (l. 1961), quietly and contritely kneels to the wife he had wronged.

From the point where Margareta and Rudolf enter, there is a marked change in the quality of the dialogue. Instead of excited talk (fears, misgivings, expectations and plans for revenge) we now meet a much more even emotion—Margareta's grief—and she relates the story of her woes in long speeches, using a great variety of words suggestive of misery and lifelessness, as in the following passage:

> Wer hieß den Muntern denn zur Freite gehn
> Bei der unselgen Königin der Tränen,
> Zum Grab gebeugt durch all der Ihren Tod?

> Seitdem mit diesen Augen ich gesehn,
> Im grausen Kerker von Apulien
> Den römschen König Heinrich, meinen Gatten,
> Des harten Friedrich allzuweichen Sohn,
> Von nahverwandten Händen liegen tot,
> Und tot die beiden hoffnungsvollen Kleinen,
> Die ihm mein Schoß, seitdem verschlossen, trug;
> War Lust ein Fremdling dieser öden Brust,
> Und Lächeln floh entsetzt von meinen Lippen,
> Die Gram und Schmerz mit seinem Siegel schloß.
>
> (ll. 243–55)

Another passage where a mood or state of mind is conveyed by piling up different words that indicate it is Ottokar's indictment of the laziness, inactivity and hand-to-mouth living of the Bohemians, whom he regards as much inferior to the Germans he is trying to introduce:

> Ich weiß wohl, was ihr mögt, ihr alten Böhmen:
> Gekauert sitzen in verjährtem Wust,
> Wo kaum das Licht durch blinde Scheiben dringt;
> Verzehren, was der vorge Tag gebracht,
> Und ernten, was der nächste soll verzehren,
> Am Sonntag Schmaus, am Kirmeß plumpen Tanz,
> Für alles andre taub und blind. (ll. 468–74)

It is a notable achievement that this first Act provides not only a clear account of the many facts relevant to the complicated historical conditions, but also contains such poetry. There are, of course, few images (about 15 in 800 lines of the Act). With so much exposition of historical detail they cannot abound, for a simile or metaphor constitutes a retarding element, holding up the action or narrative while one thing is compared or equated with another. Grillparzer's similes often extend over six or more lines, but not in those plays or sections of plays where the action is swift or where a great variety of detail has to be given. The images of *König Ottokar* are striking, but fantastic imagery would be out of place in the concrete situations of historical drama, and Grillparzer reserves it for his plays for the popular stage.

Margareta stresses not only her grief but also Ottokar's injustice. She says of his desire for an heir from a new marriage:

"Doch was soll Erbrecht, das aus Unrecht stammt?" (l. 214).
And of his plans to divorce her:

> Er handelt unrecht, unerlaubt an mir   (l. 237)
>
> .   .   .   .   .
>
> Er soll vor Unrecht sorglich sich bewahren.   (l. 380)

Ottokar has seen all his enemies yield to him and now expects the
law to do so, and his plans to divorce Margareta constitute his
first attempt to tamper with it. The legal arguments with which he
supports his divorce petition are laughable; "der König spottet"
says Margareta, when she hears them. And at heart he cares
nothing for the legality of his action, and says bluntly: "Der
König ist, der Königinnen macht!" (l. 643). Margareta's complaint
against him is not a personal one, otherwise she would not
intercede for him, as she later does. What she is resisting is the
annulling of the legal bond:

> Der König sende heute noch mich fort,
> Ich will ihm danken, wie ich nie gedankt!
> Doch soll er mir die Ehe nicht betasten,
> Beflecken nicht das Band, das uns vereint.   (ll. 286–9)

Rudolf's behaviour towards him is just as impersonal. In Act III,
for instance, he does everything to avoid a personal triumph over
him. Thus Ottokar must take the fiefs kneeling as this is required
by law: yet he can kneel in the seclusion of the tent to avoid any
humiliation. Even in the first scene of the play, Rudolf speaks as
the disinterested champion of law, saying to Margareta that
Austria and Styria are "Reichslehen" to which Ottokar has no
right if he divorces her. This respect for the claims of the Empire
must be an impersonal regard for law and order, for Rudolf is not
yet Emperor and does not expect to be elected. Like Margareta
he is prepared to be Ottokar's friend if only the king will respect
the law. Margareta's concern with law and stability has been clear
from the first, for it was to restore order in her own country after
the unrest following the death of the last of the Babenbergs that
she agreed to marry Ottokar. The conflict in the play is reducible
to Ottokar versus the law.

From the beginning of the second scene, with the exception of Ottokar's report of the victory he has just won, talk of the past is over, and the dialogue is concentrated on his plans for the present and future. Martial pomp and splendour mark his entry, and his armour is a good example of how much Grillparzer can convey by visible means. It shows that he has just returned from battle and also his consciousness of his own achievements as conqueror. When he begins to lay it aside, he illustrates his violence and impatience. The stage directions tell that he "reißt selbst gewaltsam die Schiene ab und wirft sie mitten in den Saal". Other visible stage properties in this scene are the sword of the Tartars (what he says as he handles it typifies his contemptuous attitude to his subjects) and the coat he shows to the mayor of Prague as a demonstration of the superiority of German workmanship. Then ducal coronets are brought by Austrian and Styrian nobles and offered submissively to him. Both deputations address Margareta as his queen as they enter, and make a particular point of doing homage to her, thus preparing us for their defection from him once he has divorced her. His ruthlessness is brought out when he rudely orders them to act as witnesses to his repudiation of her. Next, the Carinthians bring another coronet, and all three are visible signs of the power in which he glories, as is clear when he says to the Carinthians:

> Fügt eure Krone dort zu jenen beiden,
> Und laßt mich freun des königlichen Anblicks. (ll. 674–5)

He makes no attempt to conceal his pleasure at the death of an uncle which has brought him this further crown. His ruthlessness is well expressed in the terse line: "Ich gehe meinen Gang, was hindert, fällt" (l. 636), and in the repetition and near-alliteration of his words:

> So hoch ein Mensch mag seine Größe setzen,
> So hoch hat Ottokar gesetzt die seine. (ll. 596–7)

A final example of the exploitation of visible stage properties in this scene is the confusion between the shields decorated with the white and the red lions respectively, the emblems of Bohemia and Habsburg. The proverb that the imperial eagle would come to rest in the lion's den is historical, and it is also historical that Ottokar's supporters thought that it foretold his election. What Grillparzer has added is visible action (see ref. 22, pp. 50–1). The shield with the red lion of Habsburg is mistaken for Ottokar's and brandished as the proverb is recited.

The solemnity of the formal repudiation of Margareta (the main incident of this scene) is underlined by the slow and ponderous language of the Chancellor, who addresses her as "Erlauchte Frau and Königin Margrete" and devotes three lines of verse to her various titles before reaching his question: "Wer führt das Wort in Eurer Gnaden Sache?" He goes on to name the place where the synod which dissolved her marriage sat, its chairman and his titles—details given only to bring out the solemnity of the occasion, which is also expressed by the use of archaic words and constructions.

In this opening Act Grillparzer achieves continuous, uninterrupted and direct action. We are not told that Ottokar's behaviour has alienated the nobles, but see it happening. We are not simply told that he is divorcing Margareta; the legal proceedings are enacted before our eyes. In French classical tragedy, continuity is achieved at the expense of replacing direct action by messengers' reports. In the Elizabethan drama, on the other hand, there is direct action but often little continuity—endless changes of scene and breaks in time. Grillparzer has combined the advantages of both these types of drama, and deliberately aimed at such a synthesis— "das Leben und die Form so zu vereinigen, daß beiden ihr volles Recht geschieht" (II, 8, 285).

Act II is another achievement in continuity and consists of a single unbroken scene, the central section of which contains the most important developments—the news of Rudolf's election and Ottokar's reaction to it. The Act begins and ends quietly with Zawisch's serenading, while the central section is, in contrast, very animated and ends with the king and his followers rushing "tumultuarisch" to the hunt. In Zawisch's opening monologue (one of the few in the play) he affects passion for Kunigunde and tells of the defection of the Austrians—another indication of the consequences of Ottokar's behaviour to Margareta. Zawisch does not, of course, say in so many words that he is pretending to love Kunigunde in order to thwart Ottokar, but only "Ich bin verliebt! O weh, mein Herz ist fort!" followed by his usual cynical laughter, so that no direct statement of motive is necessary.

When Kunigunde enters, her first speech shows how sharp-tongued she is, and it is her wicked tongue that later goads Ottokar into breaking faith with Rudolf. Her very style brings out her acerbity—there are often breaks within a line as well as at its end, and the effect of jerkiness is enhanced by repetition. In this way her speech is divided into short, sharp phrases:

> Ich weiß nicht, Herr, bin ich nicht voll bei Sinnen,
> War ich im Fiebertraum, die Tage her;
> Wie, oder seid Ihr ganz so unverschämt,
> So rasend—Nein! Die Sprache hat kein Wort!
> Verrückung möcht am ersten es bezeichnen—
> So unverschämt-verrückt, als Ihr Euch zeigt?
> Bei meiner Ankunft schriet Ihr gellend auf—
> *Ihr* warts! Ich stand drei Schritte fern und *weiß* es!
> Seitdem verfolgt Ihr rastlos mich mit Blicken,
> Mit Blicken, die ich näher nicht bezeichne,
> Doch regt sich mir der Ingrimm, denk ich dran.   (ll. 869–79)

There could be no greater contrast with Margareta's long, smooth sentences, where three or four lines may run on without break or pause.

One function of this second Act is to motivate Kunigunde's infidelity. She is represented as a person who follows her own desires without inhibitions; she is dissatisfied with her position as Ottokar's wife which leaves her no authority of her own, and she finds him too old to interest her. Her ambition to be queen had led her to stifle her feelings for the Hungarian nobleman she had loved, and now that she finds she is more of a menial than a queen, she naturally turns to Zawisch, who reminds her of him. A clear indication of her attraction to Zawisch comes after he has stolen the "Schleife" from her arm. She cries out to Ottokar "Ha, mein Gemahl!", clearly intending to complain of Zawisch's improper behaviour. If she were to proceed his life would be forfeit, but she first looks to see whether he shows any sign of fear. The stage directions tell of a "Pause, während welcher die Königin Zawisch ansieht, der, ruhig vor sich hinblickend dasteht". This courage obviously impresses her, for with sudden decision she turns to Ottokar and instead of indicting Zawisch, asks a pointless question: "Geht Ihr noch heut nach Ribnik auf die Jagd?" (l. 1064). This situation, where one character is at first hostile and then friendly to another, is a stock one in drama, and the problem for the dramatist is to convey the change of heart. Grillparzer's method is to use few words but rather gestures at the crucial moments.

As in the first Act, there is much direct action. We are indeed told of the defection of Ottokar's supporters (e.g. by Zawisch in his opening monologue), but we also see it happening (the incident of Merenberg's escape). Again, we are told that Ottokar is a tyrant (by the heralds of the Empire) but we also see him acting as one; and that his behaviour illuminates the statement of the heralds is underlined when one of them says to him, commenting on the mass arrests he has ordered:

> Der Auftritt hier erspart mir die Erklärung,
> Warum die Fürsten, Herr, nicht Euch gewählt. (ll. 1280–1)

The one thing that cannot be directly portrayed in this Act is Rudolf's election. Ottokar's Chancellor, who, we know, has been at Frankfurt to watch the election (l. 1187) comes in wringing his hands, a gesture that betrays at once that Ottokar has not been elected. And instead of allowing the Chancellor to tell the details, Grillparzer has them communicated in a more direct way, introducing the heralds of the Empire for this purpose.

I have already noted that there are few monologues in this play. It is, of course, easy for the dramatist to dispense with them if he concentrates on outer action. But Grillparzer can communicate thoughts and emotions without resort to the monologue, and a striking example occurs at this point. Ottokar, confident that he himself will be chosen, stands holding a letter from his Chancellor which names men, who, he thinks, are intriguing against him. He points to their names and shouts to the ambassador of the "Reich" that they must be deposed once he is elected: "Die müssen fort." But then he hears his Chancellor tell Zawisch that Rudolf has been elected, and the stage directions read: "Ottokar fährt zusammen; die Hand, mit der er auf den Brief zeigt, beginnt zu zittern; er stottert noch einige Worte." He goes on to point to another name and to say, but now in a very half-hearted manner: "und der—muß fort!" (l. 1220). When a character receives news that gives him a great shock, a dramatist will normally express this emotion either by miming or by declamation. With either method, exaggeration will give ludicrous effects. Schiller's early dramas give examples enough. We may think of Ferdinand's gestures at the end of *Kabale und Liebe*, when he learns that Luise is innocent. He stands "starr und einer Bildsäule gleich, in langer toter Pause hingewurzelt, fällt endlich wie von einem Donnerschlag nieder". Ferdinand is, it must be admitted, feeling the effects of the poison as well as the shock of Luise's disclosure. Nevertheless, the very restraint of Ottokar's gestures—he merely stutters his instructions instead of giving them in his usual manner—enhances their effectiveness.

Ottokar breaks down here because he was not expecting opposition, as has been stressed repeatedly. Thus he says:

> Ich hauche—und wo war dann Rosenberg? (l. 1135)
>
> . . . . .
>
> Hier ist das Reich! (l. 1144)

And in l. 1182 he sees himself as a second Charlemagne. Much of his success has been sheer good fortune. His victory over the Hungarians was largely due to Rudolf's decisive cavalry attack, and his large empire has been acquired by marriage or inheritance. But once he has been raised up by such fortuities, his position goes to his head, and he attributes his power to personal qualities which make him invincible. Nowhere is this clearer than in Act III, scene 2, where he admits that the military advantages are with Rudolf, yet is convinced that, against the great Ottokar, Rudolf must surely lose:

> *Zawisch.* Die Feinde sind im Nachteil, das ist klar!
> *Ottokar.* Das ist *nicht* klar! Die Wage steht für sie.
> Der einzige Vorteil—doch der soll entscheiden!—
> Ist, das Euch Ottokar, und jene Habsburg führt. (ll. 1542–5)

Ottokar's career is tragic because circumstances have brought out the unpleasant traits in a man who, in different circumstances, might well have behaved more wisely and justly.* Even now his character is far from black. His despotism in driving the Bohemians from Prague masks a creditable zeal for social reform.† That before he acquired great power he was a wise and just king is alluded to (ll. 1560–6).‡ And Grillparzer has certainly made him morally better than the historical Ottokar, who tortured old Merenberg barbarously and had Milota's brother Benesch burned alive.§

In the final scene of the third Act Rudolf and Ottokar are confronted. It is always good theatre to bring antagonists face to face to argue their differences, as Schiller realized when he deviated from history in order to confront the queens in *Maria Stuart*. The previous scene shows Ottokar gradually reaching the

---

*This is how Grillparzer himself conceived Ottokar, whom he compared with Napoleon: "Beide . . . Eroberer, ohne eigentliche Bösartigkeit, durch die Umstände zur Härte, wohl gar zur Tyrannei fortgetrieben." Cf. his reference to Ottokar's "ursprüngliche Gutartigkeit" and his note: "Ottokar, der Übermuth, der Wahnsinn des Glückes, der nur sich selbst sieht und in der ganzen Welt das Werkzeug" (quoted by Klaar[22, pp. 4, 119]).

†The social motive underlying the replacement of Bohemians by Germans was not suggested in the historical works available to Grillparzer, although later historians imputed it to Ottokar.[22, p. 44] This is often given as proof that Grillparzer understood history better than the historians of his day (cf. below, p. 105). But his concern was not to reach a profound understanding of history, but to find motives for his hero's behaviour that will command sympathy.

‡Klaar says[22, p. 71] that in these lines Grillparzer has drawn on "die vielen historischen Berichte über Ottokars civilisatorische Wirksamkeit".

§Ref. 22, pp. 21–3, 90, 120.

state of mind in which he is prepared to meet Rudolf, but the first scene of the Act seems almost superfluous. To devote a special scene to the capture of old Merenberg has the effect of breaking the Act into episodes, so that the continuity which characterized the previous ones is lost.

It was perhaps the mummery of this scene (with knights in full armour with their visors closed, silently answering questions with a shake of the head) that led Carlyle to classify this play as a mere "Ritterschauspiel" with pageantry but little character-drawing (see below, p. 105). But although the scene could be cut without blurring the action, it is easy to understand why Grillparzer was anxious to have old Merenberg's capture enacted. It is the ill-treatment meted out to him that provokes his son Seyfried into killing Ottokar, and the events which lead indirectly to the death of the hero are too important to be merely reported.

Grillparzer's care over the motivation of details is well illuminated in this first scene. Merenberg admits the two knights because he hopes that they may bring him news of his son and because he feels that to shut himself up would arouse suspicion. He also derives some sense of security from having twenty of his own men within the castle gates. Grillparzer is then careful to explain (ll. 1415–18) how it is none the less possible for the two to capture him.

In scene 2 we return to Ottokar. His confidence in himself is unshaken, he still lards his speeches with oaths and bangs on the table to assert himself. But although his character has not yet changed, his situation has, and his very first speech shows that he is faced with defection. The main function of the scene is to motivate his decision to meet Rudolf. It would be quite out of character for him to willingly humble himself, and so Grillparzer makes him regard the meeting as an opportunity for humiliating Rudolf. Although he has just admitted that the military advantage is with Rudolf, he is convinced that the Emperor has invited him because he feels his own weakness ("Die Schwäche macht versöhnlich"), and he envisages Rudolf fumbling for words in his presence—a fine piece of irony.

From Ottokar's Chancellor, we learn that by his prudence and firmness Rudolf has restored peace and order:

> Die Ruh ist hergestellt im weiten Deutschland,
> Die Räuber sind bestraft, die Fehden ruhn.
> Die Fürsten einig und ihm eng verbunden;
> Der Papst für ihn; im Land nur eine Stimme. (ll. 1485–9)

Here again is the familiar contrast: Rudolf representing peace and order, Ottokar war and chaos. Under Rudolf "die Fehden ruhn", whereas Ottokar, we learn in the next scene, is waging a feud with the Archbishop of Salzburg and laying waste his territory. In this passage too the Pope is mentioned for the first time, almost as an afterthought. In history, papal backing or opposition played a decisive role in the fortunes of both Rudolf and Ottokar. But this was naturally ignored by Grillparzer, who evidently wished to stress the former's reliance on law and the latter's arrogance. The contrast between the two rulers is well seen in scene 3, where Rudolf unpretentiously performs the simple task of mending his own helmet, whereas the arrogant Ottokar enters in all his finery, "in glänzender Rüstung, darüber einen bis auf die Fersen gehenden reichgestickten Mantel; statt des Helmes die Krone auf dem Haupte".

Before this entry Ottokar von Horneck, whom Grillparzer took for the author of the rhymed chronicle of Austria,* one of his sources, is introduced to deliver a long speech in praise of Austria and its people:

> O gutes Land! O Vaterland! Inmitten
> Dem Kind Italien und dem Manne Deutschland,
> Liegst du, der wangenrote Jüngling da. (ll. 1699–1701)

The profusion of imagery makes the speech stand out as a retarding element. The pretext for von Horneck's appearance is that he has come to urge Rudolf to see that Ott von Lichtenstein, his feudal lord, is released from captivity by Ottokar. It is in pleading for his lord that he is led to praise Austrians in general:

---

*See Ehrhard.[11, p. 323] I am indebted to his account of the play on a number of points.

Rudolf. Wer seid ihr?
von Horneck. Ottokar von Horneck, Dienstmann
    Des edlen Ritters Ott von Lichtenstein
    Den König Ottokar samt andern Landherrn,
    Ohn Recht und Urteil hält in enger Haft.
    O, nehmt Euch sein, nehmt Euch des Landes an!   (ll. 1666–70)

He does not again mention his "Herr" but devotes the next thirty lines to his "Land".

It would be unfair to criticize Grillparzer for not adhering to standards which he did not recognize. But when we find him saying that Goethe was, as a dramatist, "durchaus ohne Belang" because of his habit of introducing speeches which are, dramatically, not to the point, then we are surely entitled to complain when he does the very same thing. In the passage criticizing Goethe he says:

Zum dramatischen Dialog ist . . . nicht genug, daß verschiedene Personen abwechselnd sprechen, sondern das, was sie sagen, muß unmittelbar aus ihrer gegenwärtigen Lage, aus ihrer gegenwärtigen Leidenschaft hervorgehen, jedes Wort muß überdies eine unverkennbare Richtung nach dem Zwecke des Stückes oder der Scenen haben. (II, 7, 106.)

Of these two requirements he has, in Horneck's speech, broken both. It is not intelligible in the light of Horneck's state of mind and situation that he should say what he does. He is supposed to be worried about his lord, but devotes only four lines to him and more than thirty to Austria. Neither can it be said that his words advance the action or explain anything we need to know about the situation or the characters. They are never referred to again, and von Horneck is obviously introduced into the play only to pronounce them, for as soon as he has done so he is dismissed from it. We may compare him with Shakespeare's John of Gaunt who speaks of England as:

> This royal throne of kings, this sceptered isle,
> This earth of Majesty, this seat of Mars,
> This other Eden, demi-paradise . . .

But John of Gaunt is at least an integral part of the play in which he appears.

Before Ottokar enters, Rudolf promises Seyfried that his father, now Ottokar's prisoner, will be freed. Grillparzer is careful never to let us lose sight of the Merenbergs (because of the important part they play in bringing about Ottokar's death) and makes skilful use of Seyfried in this third Act. Ottokar's words to him as he enters (ll. 1723–4) show that he is so sure of victory over Rudolf that he is already planning revenge against Seyfried for deserting him. And when at the end of the Act, Seyfried approaches him with what is presumably a humble request to free his father from captivity, Ottokar realizes that the man he hates for being the first to set an example as a deserter to the other Styrians, has witnessed his humiliation. And so, instead of listening to him, he rushes off to hide his shame, which is compressed into one word "Fort!"—the last of the Act. His shame is revealed here primarily by miming, as he tears the crown from his head and pulls open the straps of his coat so that this "bis auf die Fersen gehender reichgestickter Mantel" lies now in the dust.

Ottokar is brought to kneel to Rudolf after Rudolf's military superiority has been shown as the mayor of Vienna lays the keys of the city at his feet, the commander of one of Ottokar's garrisons is led in captive, and Milota brought on in chains. The capture of Milota is Grillparzer's invention (see ref. 22, p. 66 n), and the confrontation of Ottokar with his captured commander gives an effective stage picture, like the equally fictitious confrontation of Margareta and Kunigunde in Act I. The nobles of Austria and Styria then raise their colours on the Emperor's side of the stage, showing how Ottokar has alienated these provinces. Rudolf analyses the cause of Ottokar's ruthless behaviour:

> Ihr wart ein mächtger Fürst, ein großer König,
> Eh die Gelegenheit des Mehrbesitzes
> In Euch entzündet auch den Wunsch dazu. (ll. 1881–3)

He himself might well have become an Ottokar, for he says of his youth:

> An Fremden und Verwandten, Freund und Feind
> Übt ich der raschen Tatkraft jungen Arm,
> Als wär die Welt ein weiter Schauplatz nur
> Für Rudolf und sein Schwert. (ll. 1895–8)

The difference in character between the two men is not one of original endowment—as youths they were friends and delighted in the same things—but derives from their different experience. Ottokar's acquisition of territory brought out the worst in him, while Rudolf as Emperor has little material power: all the princes are richer than he (l. 1798) and he can secure their support only by offering them peace and justice. He has nothing but the rectitude of his principles to recommend him. Continuing the story of his life, he says that after his turbulent youth:

> Da nahm mich Gott mit seiner starken Hand
> Und setzte mich auf jene Thronesstufen,
> Die aufgerichtet stehn ob einer Welt,
>
> . . . . .
>
> So fiels wie Schuppen ab von meinen Augen
> Und all mein Ehrgeiz war mit eins geheilt. (ll. 1904–11)

This long story enables us to see him as a less perfect and therefore more human figure, capable of wrongdoing, and shows the power of circumstances in shaping character—something essential to our understanding of Ottokar's tragedy.

Rudolf continues with lines which bring out the historical perspective of the play:

> Der Jugendtraum der Erde ist geträumt. (l. 1914)
>
> . . . . .
>
> Wir stehn am Eingang einer neuen Zeit. (l. 1920)

He says too that the heroic age is over; "Der Helden, der Gewaltgen Zeit dahin" (l. 1916). Grillparzer's original title for the play was "Eines Gewaltigen Glück und Ende". As "ein Gewaltiger" Ottokar is out of step with the times. Under the old code might was right; under the new, peace replaces war, debate aggression. Ottokar is an atavistic survival of the old order, trying to impose it on a world that is outgrowing it.

This situation, in which tragedy is enacted at a period of transition in world ethics, is more often found in Hebbel's plays than in Grillparzer's. It is an integral part of Hebbel's theory of tragedy that the action should take place when old values are declining but new ones not completely established. The tragic hero, in clinging to the old—or in championing the new—comes into conflict with his human environment. Meister Anton, for instance, ruthlessly imposes the standards of his generation on the next which does not cherish them, and Herodes, who believes that he may use everyone as a means to his own ends, is for this reason brought into conflict with the society in which he lives, which regards each individual as sacrosanct. Herzog Albrecht and Demetrius are equally uncompromising in their adherence to views which are ethically ahead of their day and age. Hebbel's tragic heroes must necessarily be aggressive—men who believe in their own ideas so strongly that they are incapable of modifying them or sometimes even of seeing that there are other points of view. It was for this reason that he disliked conciliatory endings, which are only possible if the hero defers to other views. Grillparzer's heroes, on the other hand, are rarely as aggressive as Ottokar, and even he only becomes so because he acquires a great empire. Consequently, when it is stripped from him, he is able to see the error of his ways.

The fourth Act consists of a single, unbroken scene. What Milota says at the beginning illuminates his character and motives:

> Wär nicht das ganze Land mit ihm beschimpft,
> Ich wollte lachen, wie einst Zawisch lachte.   (ll. 2018–19)

Thus unlike Zawisch, who subordinates everything to his hatred of Ottokar, Milota is primarily a Bohemian patriot, and will even forgive the king's behaviour to Berta if he will now rule with the help of Bohemian nobles and cease favouring Germans. That Ottokar encouraged German settlers not only motivates Milota's final betrayal of his king, but also illuminates a positive facet of Ottokar, for his aim was to encourage the development in his own country of the skills and culture practised in Germany (l. 484–90, 505).

When Milota leaves Ottokar comes "in einen dunklen Mantel gehüllt, ein schwarzes Barett mit schwarzen Federn tief in die Augen gedrückt"—a marked contrast, then, with the glittering apparel he wore in Act III to overawe Rudolf. He converses with his servant by pantomime. The stage directions indicate that "Ottokar schüttelt das Haupt", "Der König lacht höhnisch auf", "Ottokar stampft ungeduldig mit dem Fuße". As in Act IV of *Ein Bruderzwist*, the hero's loss of power is made clear without words. Ottokar's very silence, apart from his dress and gestures, is eloquent enough, for in his days of triumph, as Kunigunde is soon to point out, "reden konnt er, groß und fürstlich reden!" (l. 2145).

When his servant leaves him, Ottokar's monologue (like all the previous ones in the play) conveys the emotion dominant in the speaker, in this case shame. Here, in his first quiet and unaggressive speech, he contrasts his former splendour with his present insignificance. Addressing his own castle, the gate of which is visible on the stage, he decides that he is too dishonoured to enter, but must sit as his own gate-keeper. Once again ideas and emotions, being thus linked with something we can see, gain in vividness. In the whole long opening section of Act IV he speaks only when alone. When Kunigunde and Zawisch leave him his sense of shame is compressed into two lines. He feels he is no more than a shadow:

> Ist das mein Schatten?—Nun, zwei Könige!
> Man kommt, man naht! Wohin verberg ich mich? (ll. 2201–2)

Kunigunde's speeches wound him most. One of her principal functions in the play is to goad him here into breaking the treaty with Rudolf, and after this episode she plays little further part.

The final section of Act IV shows Ottokar's reassertion of his authority. Here Grillparzer arouses sympathy for his hero by having him treated unjustly, for the imperial herald does not put Rudolf's case as he himself would have done, but delights in exploiting the weakness of Ottokar's position. Our sympathy grows when Ottokar humbly obeys his imperious demands, promises to free the hostages and to evacuate Austria. But under further provocation his restraint breaks down. And when the herald leaves the stage, everyone rushes after him, leaving Ottokar alone with his Chancellor—a visual picture of his loss of power and authority which is underlined when he asks his Chancellor: "Bist du mein ganzer Hof?" While the Chancellor goes to recall the herald, Ottokar ponders whether to swallow these insults or die reasserting his authority. Here for the first time in the play Grillparzer uses the monologue for deliberation, and Ottokar's decision to defy Rudolf shapes the whole remaining action.

In Schiller's plays too one of the principals often has a deliberative monologue in the fourth Act to express a psychological conflict and its resolution in a decision crucial for the rest of the action. Elisabeth (Act IV, scene 10) finally makes up her mind to sign Maria's death warrant, and Tell (Act IV, scene 3) resolves to kill Gessler. But Grillparzer handles this dramatic device more concisely. Elisabeth's monologue continues for sixty lines, Tell's for ninety, Ottokar's for only fourteen. We saw earlier that Grillparzer reacted sharply against the lengthy declamation so characteristic of Schiller's style (see above, p. 3).

After this monologue Ottokar reverts to his former style. It is he who now takes the initiative in the conversation, interrupting the herald, and snatching Rudolf's letter from his hand. When he asks the queen whether he is to tear it up and renew the war, she replies:

> An Eurem Sarge will ich lieber stehn,
> Als mit Euch liegen, zugedeckt von Schande! (ll. 2401-2)

He comments "So stark? Ein Tröpflein Milde täte wohl!" In the next Act we shall see many other indications that he is no longer capable of his former ruthlessness. But Kunigunde renews her taunts, and in tearing the letter Ottokar gives visible expression to his determination to fight to the death.

His former drive and energy have, however, gone, and in Act V Füllenstein complains of his overcautious tactics. His confident pose is belied when he shivers in the coldness of the morning: "'s ist kalt! Hat niemand einen Mantel?" (l. 2584). We are reminded of the Tempelhüter's anxiety, expressed in his final monologue with: "Mich schaudert. Weh! Hätt' ich mein Oberkleid!" (See above, p. 78.)

The final Act is in many ways unlike the others. Its five scenes, culminating in the battle in which Ottokar is killed, give an episodic effect which impairs continuity without increasing the pace. And Ottokar's monologue in the final scene is far longer than any other in the play. He dwells on the wondrousness of human life, underlining the magnitude of his own guilt in sacrificing men by the thousand for his own aggrandizement:

> Den Menschen, den du hingesetzt zur Lust,
> Ein Zweck, ein Selbst, im Weltall eine Welt—
> Gebaut hast du ihn als ein Wunderwerk,
> Mit hoher Stirn und aufgericht'tem Nacken,
> Gekleidet in der Schönheit Feierkleid
> Und wunderbar mit Wundern ihn umringt.
> Er hört und sieht und fühlt und freut sich.
> Die Speise nimmt er auf in seinen Leib,
> Da treten wirkende Gewalten auf,
> Und weben fort und fort mit Fasern und Gefäß
> Und zimmern ihm sein Haus; kein Königsschloß
> Mag sich vergleichen mit dem Menschenleib!
> Ich aber hab sie hin zu Tausenden geworfen,
> Um einer Torheit, eines Einfalls willen,
> Wie man den Kehricht schüttet vor die Tür. (ll. 2834–48)

Here as so often in Grillparzer's fifth Acts, the emphasis is on comment and reflection, and striking images, absent from those parts of the play filled with action, return. It has often been observed that this whole passage was written with Napoleon very much in mind. His career had only recently ended, and we saw that Grillparzer was struck by similarities between him and Ottokar.

Finally Rudolf addresses his two sons in the same manner that Bancbanus finally addresses the child who will one day be king— urging them to eschew what has disfigured the monarch who has dominated the play:

> Doch solltet ihr je übermütig werden,
> Mit Stolz erheben euren Herrscherblick,
> So denkt an den Gewaltigen zurück,
>
> .   .   .   .   .
>
> An Ottokar, sein Glück und an sein Ende!

This is not intended as trite moralizing. In both plays the effect is to bring us to survey and reflect on the whole that is here brought to a close.

Rudolf's speech also includes a glimpse of the glorious future of the House of Habsburg in Austria, giving a bright conclusion—patriotically inspired—very different from the melancholy pessimism with which Grillparzer's previous plays had closed. And never again was he to conclude a tragedy on such an optimistic note.

Grillparzer's comments on *König Ottokar* express his views concerning the adaptation of historical facts for dramatic purposes. In his autobiography he stresses that nearly all the events in the play are authenticated by history, or at any rate by legend, and says that he took considerable pains to study source material so as not to be obliged to invent incidents. For, he adds, the poet chooses historical themes to give the extraordinary events of his play "eine Konsistenz, einen Schwerpunkt der Realität. . . . Alexander der Große oder Napoleon als erdichtete Personen würden der Spott aller Vernünftigen sein." But Grillparzer had no sympathy for the exact reproduction of historical detail that the Romantic writers were advocating[50, p. 42], and which had led to a large number of pageant-like plays with little delineation of character. And so he continues the passage by denying that a poet need abide by "das eigentlich Historische . . ., nämlich das wirklich Wahre, nicht bloß der Ereignisse, sondern auch der Motive und Entwicklungen". It is obvious enough that he was perfectly prepared to simplify the historical facts for the sake of condensation and clarity, and also to reinterpret the motives of his hero so that some sympathy is enlisted for him (see above, p. 94). Furthermore, his patriotism also prompted him to such reinterpretation. Susceptibility to patriotic motive is something he did share with the Romantics, and so he declared:

> Wenn . . . aus dem Untergange Ottokars die
> Gründung der habsburgischen Dynastie in Österreich
> hervorging, so war das für einen österreichischen
> Dichter eine unbezahlbare Gottesgabe. (I, 16, 166–7)

Even Redlich, who stresses the accuracy of Grillparzer's portrayal of historical characters, admits that his Rudolf I is sketched "in etwas idealisierten Zügen". But he goes on to claim that

Grillparzer had greater insight than the historians of his day and in some cases anticipated the findings of their successors. One of his examples is the portrait of Rudolf II in *Ein Bruderzwist* which, he says, is "in wesentlichen Zügen" identical with that given much later by von Stieve.* In actual fact Stieve attributes a number of the Emperor's most important acts (utilized in the play) to his fanatical Catholicism, boundless egoism and thirst for revenge,† whereas Grillparzer ascribed the same behaviour to motives which make him an unselfish statesman of extraordinary insight. Apart from the obvious factor of patriotism, Grillparzer was understandably anxious to portray a hero with whom we can sympathize.

In both *Ottokar* and *Ein Bruderzwist* Grillparzer includes much historical detail (as the Romantics did), but nevertheless makes these plays essentially character tragedies, not plays of outer action or mere pageantry. In *Ein Bruderzwist* (as we shall see) he works with a large canvas—many characters and outer action that includes battles and revolution—and portrays the political situation at the beginning of the Thirty Years' War in considerable detail. Yet all this is subordinated to what is happening in the minds of Rudolf and Mathias, wherein the tragedy really lies. In *König Ottokar* the very wealth of historical detail given in direct action made Carlyle blind to its portrayal of character—to the obvious differences in character between Ottokar and Rudolf, Margareta and Kunigunde, Zawisch and Milota, and so on. For he declared that although the play is replete with "coronation-ceremonies, Hungarian dresses, whiskered halberdiers, alarms of battle and the pomp and circumstance of glorious war", yet the characters differ "in dress and name only", and not "in nature and mode of being."[7, pp. 329–30]

---

*Redlich.[37, pp. 20, 23] His judgement has been endorsed by Craig Houston [9, pp. 19–22] and by Sengle.[43, p. 107]

†According to Stieve [48] Rudolf II regarded the war against the Turks as a Crusade that was to bring him immortal fame, and refused to terminate it because of his "überspannte Auffassung des Kaiserthums und krankhaftes Ehrgefühl". Stieve also writes of his "grimmige, sich zuletzt jeder vernünftigen Erwägung verschließende Rachgier, womit er Antastungen . . . seines Ansehens . . . und seiner Gewalt nachtrug und zu vergelten suchte".

2. Ein Bruderzwist in Habsburg

Ein Bruderzwist is one of the three plays that Grillparzer completed after *Weh dem, der lügt!* and withheld from publication
during his lifetime. It is a study of the conditions which culminated
in the outbreak of the Thirty Years' War in 1618. I will begin with
a brief account of the historical facts on which he drew.*

From 1576 Rudolf II was Holy Roman Emperor, and also ruler
of Austria, Hungary and Bohemia. He, his brothers—Archdukes
Max (who ruled Tyrol) and Mathias†—and his cousin Archduke
Ferdinand (ruler of Styria) were all Catholics, whereas many of
their subjects were Protestants, and the fact that subjects and
rulers were divided on the great question of the day was a constant
source of friction. The Protestant cause was strongly held by the
nobles, many of whom had embraced it in order to "secularize",
i.e. confiscate, Church estates. Since the nobles tended to be
Protestant, the court party saw its own interests to lie in strength-
ening the authority of the Emperor and the Catholic institutions
to which he was committed. In consequence Protestants were
persecuted, particularly in Hungary where an imperial army was
available because of the war against the Turks. Ranke has said
that this persecution was not initiated by Rudolf, and was quite
foreign to his nature, although on the other hand he was not the
man to take firm action against the Catholic party at court. It
was also easy to hoodwink him, since he hated (and so neglected)
the business of governing, was afraid to give audiences because of
the danger of assassination, and devoted himself to his interests
in art, alchemy and astrology.

Rudolf, then, allowed the Catholic party to pursue its severe
policy in Hungary, even though he was trying to maintain a
balance of strength of the two confessions in Germany. Neither
policy was successful, since there was a strong Protestant majority
in Hungary and a Catholic one in Germany. Rudolf's failure to
control these forces seems to have made him despair of taking any

*My account is based on refs. 16, 36, 39, 48.
†I adopt this spelling throughout, although "Matthias" is also common.

effective action, although he was unwilling to abdicate or delegate his powers.

The result of the severity of the Catholic court party was a rebellion by the Hungarian nobles, who joined forces with the Turks. Since Rudolf did nothing to meet this new danger, the archdukes met at Linz (April 1605) and decided to urge him to put Mathias in charge in Hungary and also to nominate his own successor. This latter request he refused, but he did reluctantly agree (October 1605) to give Mathias full authority to make peace with the Hungarian rebels and with the Turks. But while Mathias was attempting to achieve these aims, it became clear that Rudolf was at heart opposed to them, and so the archdukes met in Vienna (April 1606), declared him incapable of governing and held that Mathias was entitled to act in his stead. Mathias succeeded in negotiating a treaty with the Hungarian rebels (June 1606), the terms of which guaranteed them religious freedom, and Rudolf was then obliged to make him regent of Hungary. In November 1606 a twenty-year armistice was signed with the Turks, and Rudolf had ratified both treaty and armistice by the end of the year. However, he soon afterwards condemned Mathias' concessions as a betrayal of true religion, and hinted that his ratification was void. The result was another rebellion in Hungary (October 1607). Mathias aligned himself with the nobles there, and was joined by the nobles of Austria and Moravia. In May 1608 he marched on Prague, hoping that the Bohemian nobles would also forsake Rudolf. In this he was disappointed, for they used the occasion to extort certain privileges from Rudolf as the price of supporting him. But although Mathias failed to gain Bohemia, he compelled Rudolf to cede to him the kingdom of Hungary and the government of Austria and Moravia. Rudolf was determined to recover these territories, and his opportunity seemed to have come when they refused to recognize Mathias unless he granted them complete religious freedom. In spite of his previous support of the Protestants Mathias was a committed Catholic and closely connected with the Spanish and Papal courts. So he yielded only in Hungary, and once he had been crowned king there, he felt strong enough to offer religious freedom only to the nobles in Moravia and Austria—and not to the whole population as he had done in Hungary. This encouraged the Bohemian nobles to demand religious freedom from Rudolf, whom they compelled in 1609 to issue a "Letter of Majesty" granting toleration to all Bohemian Protestants. The following year he became reconciled with Mathias—largely through the good offices of Duke Julius of Brunswick, who travelled to and fro from Prague and Vienna many times in order to bring the two rulers to agree. Mathias recognized Rudolf as the head of the House of Austria, and agreed that Archdukes Ferdinand and Max should tender his apologies to the Emperor in Prague. But then Rudolf angered him by nominating his cousin (Ferdinand's younger brother) Archduke Leopold, Bishop of Passau, to be his successor, both as Emperor and as King of Bohemia. Leopold had won Rudolf's favour because he had not been involved in any of the archducal combinations against him, and had done his best to bring the Catholic powers (in particular Spain) to Rudolf's defence when Mathias marched on Prague in 1608. Rudolf had then commented that Leopold's plans were hot-headed, but he seems to have been moved by his loyalty. And the Catholic party much preferred Leopold to Mathias, who had compromized himself in their eyes by his dealings with Protestants. At this moment Leopold's troops in Passau broke into Austria and then into Bohemia. According to Ranke the reason for this attack is not clear. The troops were welcomed by those with Catholic sympathies, while the Protestants took fright and appealed to Mathias, who marched on Prague (March 1611) and forced Rudolf to cede Bohemia to him. Rudolf died the following year without recovering his authority.

These are the bald historical facts on which Grillparzer based the action of the first four Acts of his play. The reader will hardly find them particularly inspiring. Grillparzer certainly did not have the advantage enjoyed by Büchner when writing *Dantons Tod*—namely that a mere recital of the historical facts of his hero's career would be found moving and pathetic. To make Rudolf II appeal as a hero Grillparzer had to simplify the facts of his reign considerably, and derive his behaviour from motives with which we can sympathize. Two examples will illustrate his treatment of the material. (1) In 1606 Mathias made two peace treaties, one with the Hungarian rebels and another with the Turks. Grillparzer mentions only the latter and does not deal with the Hungarian revolt. (2) In the face of the Emperor's indecision the archdukes met twice—in Linz (1605) and Vienna (1606). Grillparzer records only one meeting which he places on the battlefield, and he restricts the business of this meeting to the question of whether to make peace with the Turks against Rudolf's wishes, whereas the archdukes were in history also concerned with the problem of the succession.

These examples also show that Grillparzer simplified the facts not only for greater clarity, but also because of his interpretation of Rudolf's character. His Rudolf sees how precarious is the equilibrium of religious and political forces, and knows that any departure from the present position, any attempt by one class or sect to gain at the expense of others is likely to lead to the most pernicious of wars. He would be quite incapable of sanctioning the kind of Catholic repression which led the Hungarian nobles to revolt, and this is one reason why Grillparzer makes no mention of any such uprising. Again, the historical Rudolf appears to have been unwilling, for reasons of religious zeal, to terminate the war against the Turks. Grillparzer's whole plot depends on retaining the historical fact of his unwillingness. But his motive had to be changed if he was to appear as a ruler of great insight, and so for Grillparzer's Rudolf the Turkish war is a necessary factor in preserving the equilibrium: it keeps his subjects from internecine doctrinal strife by uniting them against a common foe (ll. 1186 ff.). He is sure that, within generations, the fierce intolerance of the Christian confessions will abate and he sees his task to lie in preventing them from destroying each other in the present (ll. 1195–8). As a further example of Grillparzer's adaptation of the facts, I mention that the historical Rudolf was unwilling to abdicate or nominate his successor because he desired undivided

power for himself,* whereas Grillparzer's Rudolf remains in office
because he knows of no competent successor:

> Nicht daß mich lockt die stolze Herrschermacht
> Und wüßt' ich Schultern die zum Tragen tüchtig,
> Ich schüttelte sie ab als eckle Last.   (ll.1488–90)

The Rudolf of the play, then, refrains from political action
because he knows that even a slight change could cause an
explosion. He is tortured by

> das Bewußtsein, daß im Handeln,
> Ob so nun oder so, der Zündstoff liegt,
> Der diese Mine donnernd sprengt gen Himmel.   (ll. 1446–8)

He realizes that decisions, once translated into action, are irre-
vocable, and lead to consequences which cannot be foreseen with
precision, particularly when a community rather than an individual
is involved. It is not Rudolf but Thurn, the Protestant counterpart
of Klesel, who thinks that he can make his actions result in such
consequences as are desirable for him (although even he has
reservations, ll. 2213–22). Rudolf is sure of the contrary whenever
the actions are political:

> Indes der gute Mann auf hoher Stelle
> Erzittert vor den Folgen seiner Tat,
> Die als die Wirkung Eines Federstrichs
> Glück oder Unglück forterbt späten Enkeln.   (ll. 1699–1702)

His inaction is thus not caused by indifference to the fate of his
subjects—as is also clear from his quick sympathy for the victims
of Ferdinand's fanatical persecution (ll. 484–5, 498–500). And
the phrase "auf hoher Stelle" in the passage just quoted shows
that it is political action (and not necessarily other kinds of action)
concerning which he feels diffidence—although this passage has

---

*Ranke writes:[36, p. 186] "Er lebte und webte in dem Gefühl der Auto-
rität, mit der ihm der Besitz der höchsten Würde umgab. . . . Ein psycholo-
gischer Widerspruch ist es nicht, daß Rudolf die Geschäfte nicht liebte, die
ihm das Kaisertum auflegte, und sie vernachlässigte, sie aber doch auch
nicht in andere Hände gerathen lassen und den Besitz der Krone um keinen
Preis mit einem Andern theilen wollte."

often been adduced as evidence of his unwillingness to take action of any kind. In the same speech he says:

> Denn was Entschlossenheit den Männern heißt des Staats,
> Ist meisten Falls Gewissenlosigkeit.

Ruthlessness is here ascribed not to action, but to political action. But again the qualification has frequently been overlooked, and Baumann, for instance, has inferred from these lines that Rudolf subscribes to Goethe's maxim: "Der Handelnde ist immer gewissenlos: es hat niemand Gewissen als der Betrachtende." (4, p. 438) That in both passages Rudolf qualifies his statement suggests that he has in mind the obvious distinction between conscientious behaviour towards one's neighbour and conscientious political behaviour. The former can be guided by the natural instinct of sympathy, by religious teaching, or by the customs and laws of the community. But political decisions often have to be based on calculation of long-term consequences, and it is difficult to be sure even of the immediate consequences of actions which affect whole peoples. Towards one's neighbour one can cultivate good-will and not worry about the consequences of deeds which spring from this attitude. But Rudolf points out that the art of governing is very different, it is the art (Kunst):

> In der verkehrt was sonst den Menschen adelt:
> Erst der Erfolg des Wollens Wert bestimmt,
> Der reinste Wille wertlos—wenn erfolglos. (ll. 1685–7)

And while these considerations suffice to give any scrupulous statesman pause, Rudolf knows in addition that any immediate change in his particular political situation can only be for the worse:

> Zudem gibts Lagen, wo ein Schritt voraus
> Und einer rückwärts gleicherweis verderblich. (ll. 1175–6)

On his very first appearance in the play we see that Rudolf's reluctance to take political action does not in fact extend to action of other kinds. He has, it is true, even ceased to attend properly to political affairs and lives as a recluse. We see him as the Rudolf

whom Ranke had portrayed in 1832—"mürrisch, eigensinnig
argwöhnisch, empfindlich für jede Zugluft der Welt".* His
ministers try to interest him in state affairs, but he remains absorbed
in a work of literature. Some minutes pass before he speaks a
coherent sentence, and this is evoked by the book he is reading,
not by the people in his company, whom he treats only to interjections and to bangings on the floor with his stick. But when Don
Cäsar is introduced we learn that this inattention to political
matters is not due to sheer incapacity for firm action. For when
Rudolf realizes why he has come, he at once drops his reticence
and expresses his firm resolve that Cäsar's friend Russworm shall
die because guilty of murder. Rudolf's determination to take the
necessary action makes it clear enough that he can be resolute on
a moral issue where politics are not involved. And to show that
this is so Grillparzer has here fused details concerning Russworm's
trial and execution (1606) and Rudolf's relationship with his
illegitimate son Cäsar whom (according to some authorities) he
caused to be killed in 1608 for murdering his mistress.

While the complexity and the danger of the political scene
inhibits Rudolf from trying to change it, it is nausea at the selfish
clash of sectarian interests that has led him to turn away from
politics altogether and to seek consolation in art and literature:

> Damit ich lebe muß ich mich begraben,
> Ich wäre tot, lebt' ich mit dieser Welt.   (ll. 1160–1)

He indicts the motives of the religious Reformers:

> Nein, Eigendünkel war es, Eigensucht,
> Die nichts erkennt, was nicht ihr eigenes Werk.   (ll. 336–7)

The repetition brings out his abhorrence of selfishness. It is because he sees that the Protestants seek religious freedom to increase
their political power (ll. 1231 ff.) that he refuses their faith
official recognition while he can. He tolerates them, but will not
confirm them in their heresy (ll. 1560–6). How he values unselfish

---

*Ref. 36, p. 188. I can find no evidence that Grillparzer read this work.
Redlich[37, p. 18] notes that he never mentioned either Niebuhr or Ranke.

service is emphasized by his words "des Herrn Dienst vor allem", spoken as he decides to attend the mass even though this means postponing his meeting with the nephew he loves.

Although he has good reason to find the world of affairs distasteful, there is something pathological in the vehemence of his withdrawal from it—as when he angrily repeats "allein" seven times (ll. 214–20) to be rid of those who thrust political matters upon his attention, and even (so we are told) threatens Rumpf with a dagger (ll. 1417–18). This desire for solitude is not misanthropy —he eagerly looks forward to his younger nephew's arrival at the end of Act I and speaks with great warmth to Duke Julius in Act III—but only a loathing of politics. Nevertheless, from a man in his position, inattention to the minutiae of what he knows to be a dangerous political situation must appear as culpable negligence. Grillparzer has, however, done much to mitigate his guilt. He thinks the dangers of the situation are so obvious that no one will dare to precipitate a conflict behind his back. He says in retrospect:

> Ich hielt die Welt für klug, sie ist es nicht.
> Gemartert vom Gedanken droh'nder Zukunft,
> Dacht' ich die Zeit von gleicher Furcht bewegt,
> Im weisen Zögern seh'nd die einz'ge Rettung. (ll. 2300–3)

He knows his family well enough to be confident that none of them —not even Mathias—is capable of initiating open rebellion. They will let him rule, at least in name—he does not covet the realities of power—and this will preclude radical upheaval (ll. 1166, 1286). He sees that Klesel, "jener list'ge Priester" (l. 1403) is capable of setting Mathias against him, and so he has taken what he thinks are adequate steps to keep them apart (ll. 1398–9). The historical Bishop Klesel entered the service of Mathias in 1599, and Grillparzer has exaggerated his influence in order to accentuate his master's weakness. The one serious misjudgement of which the Rudolf of the play is guilty is underestimation of the lengths to which Klesel will go in ruthless defiance of his authority. And this error is to some extent excused by the portrayal of Klesel in Act II as the master politician who will resort to any trickery to achieve his aims, and who dupes all the archdukes, including Mathias whom he professes to serve.

From Rudolf's conversation with Ferdinand in Act I we learn that he has yet another motive for political inaction. Grillparzer has here skilfully exploited the historical fact of Rudolf's interest in astrology. Ranke reminds us that both Tycho Brahe and Kepler were zealous astrologers, and so Grillparzer did not need to feel that there is any absurdity in imputing such beliefs to a man of great insight of that age. And he has made them appear appropriate in Rudolf's case by relating them to his general view of human nature. He sees in the heavenly bodies the ordered regularity that he misses in politics and which, for him, is the mark of the divine, of selfless accord with God's will:

> Der Mensch fiel ab von ihm [Gott], sie [die Sterne] aber nicht,
>
> . . . .
>
> Und wers verstünde, still zu sein wie sie,
> Gelehrig fromm, den eignen Willen meisternd,
> Ein aufgespanntes, demutvolles Ohr,
> Ihm würde leicht ein Wort der Wahrheit kund,
> Die durch die Welten geht aus Gottes Munde. (ll. 407–17)

His insistence that he has not achieved the complete purity of will and selflessness manifested in the stars is no false modesty, for we shall see that when he eventually does take political action (at the end of Act III) it is anger that impels him.

His views on right behaviour are favourably contrasted with those of Ferdinand. Both agree that it must accord with God's will and not with personal inclination. But whereas Rudolf finds it impossible to ascertain the deity's will and declares that "der Dinge tiefster Kern ist mir verschlossen" (l. 422), Ferdinand, like the fanatic of all ages, is sure he has the necessary knowledge. But if Rudolf feels he lacks it, ought this not to deter him from all action, not only (as it long does) from political action? The answer is, I think, that as a sincere and devout Christian he is in no doubt as to what God wills concerning murder and so has no hesitation in condemning Russworm and—as we shall see—Cäsar for this crime. He can, then, act firmly and unambiguously when confronted with breaches of the moral law, but no divine commandments tell him how to govern his Empire.

In Act II the scene switches to the battlefield in Hungary, and Grillparzer places in the imperial camp there the one meeting of the archdukes that he records. This is unhistorical and enables him to bring some movement into the play to contrast with the inactivity of Rudolf portrayed in Act I. Of the four archdukes Ferdinand is already familiar from Act I as a fanatical Catholic. Mathias we have seen to be ambitious but weak. It was at Klesel's instigation that he asked for an army command in Hungary (ll. 126–8) and although he can dream of power (ll. 182–4) he can achieve nothing without Klesel's guidance. Leopold has also been briefly characterized as impetuous and also unswerving in personal devotion to Rudolf. Only Max is new to us. He is "ein beleibter, wohlbehaglicher Herr" (directions after l. 661), cured of political ambition by earlier failures, and his caustic and witty remarks provide the only comic element in the play. Later, at one of its most pathetic moments he keeps the tears from his eyes with a joke (ll. 2282–3).

Like Act I, scene 2 of *König Ottokar*, the opening scene of Act II is remarkable for its wealth of direct and uninterrupted action. The defeat of the imperial troops is admittedly narrated, but the facts are told by men who have come straight from the fighting, so that something of the immediacy of direct action is retained. The stage gradually fills with soldiers, arguing about what is to be done. Then gypsies set up a canteen at the back and the soldiers go to it, leaving the front first to Klesel, who is snubbed by the three archdukes as they walk across it, and then to Leopold for his furtive conversation. The hostility of the three to Klesel, whom they regard as a dangerous influence on Mathias, will play an important part in the conference scene that follows. And Leopold's conversation concerns his recruitment of an army in Passau which, we later learn (ll. 1132–4), is to protect Rudolf from Mathias, should this prove necessary. One of the principal topics throughout the scene is whether Mathias has survived the battle. Suddenly he is said to be near, and everyone rushes to meet him, except a small group of soldiers who had been haggling about the price of their support for Don Cäsar's attack on Lukrezia's carriage. This group leaves the stage in the opposite direction from that taken by all the others, and this serves to direct our attention to their sinister purpose, which we are soon to see put into effect.

The next scene takes place inside the tent where the three archdukes confer with Mathias and Klesel. The shouts of "Vivat Mathias" with which the previous scene ended are heard off-stage outside the tent, at the beginning of this one, thus establishing continuity. Mathias is wearing the dress of a Hungarian peasant, which he takes as a fitting symbol of his shame and defeat. He declares he will not lay it aside until he has restored his reputation, but he dons another coat when it is brought—a little detail that shows how readily his resolution is undermined. He is the helpless creature of Klesel, who appears in this scene as the master politician, able to turn to account every circumstance, whether expected or not. He first tries to show Mathias the folly of continuing the war now that a third of the army has perished. But Mathias insists on "neuer, doppelstarker Angriff" to clear his shame, and with sudden decision Klesel says: "Bleibt, Herr, bei eurer Weigrung", and adds, in an aside: "Vielleicht reift unsern Anschlag grade dies" (l. 765). We learn what this "Anschlag" is when the other archdukes enter. They have come to discuss whether to make peace with the Turks behind Rudolf's back. Leopold refuses even to sit at the table at which such a treasonable proposition is discussed. Max and Ferdinand can see that to continue the war is impossible, but when Klesel invites Max to say expressly that he is for peace, he replies only: "Ei, laßt mich!" (l. 889), since he does not wish to commit himself to open rebellion. Klesel says that he too is for peace, and that since Rudolf will not honour a peace treaty, one of the archdukes must be chosen to enforce it. Max, Ferdinand and Leopold naturally suspect the truth, namely that he is trying to ensure that these powers be accorded to his master Mathias, who will then be able not only to oppose Rudolf, but to do so with the backing of the most powerful members of his family. This is in fact what Klesel had called "unsern Anschlag". He knows that the archdukes hate him and will be unwilling to increase the power of Mathias, who depends upon him. So he suggests that either Max, Ferdinand or Leopold assume the necessary authority—knowing quite well that their loyalty to Rudolf will prevent them from accepting, so that the powers will have to be offered to Mathias. Now the three archdukes are only willing to let Mathias have them because he appears to be in disagreement with Klesel, who wants peace, while Mathias wants to continue the war. As the archdukes see it, if Mathias were anxious to oust Rudolf, he would argue for peace and for power to enforce it. As he in fact argues for war, they feel confident that he is without ulterior motive. Thus Klesel, in arguing for peace while his master argues vehemently for war, has dispelled the archdukes' suspicions, and when it is finally agreed that Mathias shall have the powers to enforce a peace treaty, Max says to him:

> Warst Eines Sinnes du mit diesem Mann
> (auf Klesel zeigend)
> Ich hätte die Gewalt dir nicht gegeben.   (ll. 1056–7)

Max, then, has been duped, for we know that Klesel has been deliberately exploiting his difference of opinion with Mathias. Mathias himself is incapable of appreciating Klesel's strategy, is angry with him for his opposition, and intoxicated with the new power he has achieved.

The final scene of this second Act is impressively terse. In it are enacted the attack on Lukrezia and Prokop, the arrival of the archdukes in time to frustrate it, and their capture of Don Cäsar. Their conversation also gives their reactions to the conference and Leopold's plans for restoring power to Rudolf. Altogether, the whole Act has been crowded with action: it begins and ends with soldiers in action, and the central section—the conference scene—is extremely tense.

The next Act brings a slackening in the tempo. We meet Rudolf for the second time, busy in his laboratory—another illustration of his withdrawal from the business of governing and his pre-occupation with the things of the mind. When the preparations

for his chemical experiments are imperfectly carried out, he asks:
"Ist alles denn verworren und verkehrt?" "Alles" is emphatic.
He is contrasting the practical world of politics, where he expects
nothing but disorder and confusion, with the realm of the mind,
where he expects order. That he means the adjectives "verworren"
and "verkehrt" as a description of the world of affairs is clear from
the terms in which he described it in Act I:

> So dringt die Zeit, die wildverworrne, neue
> Durch hundert Wachen bis zu uns heran.
>
> .   .   .   .   .
>
> Deucht mirs doch manchmal grimmiges Vergnügen,
> Mit ihm [Cäsar] zu ringen, in des Argen Brust
> Die Keime aufzusuchen der Verkehrtheit,
> Die ihm geliehn so wildverworrne Welt.   (ll. 321–2, 341–4)

What he is doing in his laboratory is smelting gold to supply
medallions to a select band of "Friedensritter" whose motto is to
be "Nicht ich, nur Gott". Once again we see how high he rates
self-denial. Grillparzer has taken the historical fact of Rudolf's
interest in alchemy and used it to bring out this trait in his outlook.
We saw that he turned the historical Rudolf's interest in astrology
to the same account. And these interests lead Rudolf to withdraw
his attention from politics long enough to give Klesel and his tool
Mathias their chance. As Duke Julius tells him:

> Ihr seid verraten, hoher Herr, verkauft.
> Indes Ihr lernt, lehrt Ihr der Welt den Aufruhr,
> Der schon entfesselt tobt in Euren Städten.   (ll. 1328–30)

Julius has had to disguise himself as a stoker in the laboratory to
reach Rudolf and warn him of the ominous signs. As Rudolf is
well aware, the Protestant Duke is his most loyal subject. Both
men are far-sighted and unselfish—Rudolf significantly makes him
the first "Friedensritter"—and the warmth of their friendship
contrasts with most other personal relationships of the play. It is
from what he says to Julius that we learn of Rudolf's true person-
ality which he so often disguises by abrupt withdrawal from others.
And it is Julius who tends him as he is dying at the end of Act IV
and speaks words of truth to defend his policy in Act V. Here in

Act III we learn from Julius that Mathias has claimed the crown of Hungary and that the nobles in Austria and Moravia have welcomed him as the champion of Protestant freedom. When Rudolf realizes that Klesel is behind these moves he knows that equilibrium is no longer possible:

> Nun wohl, ihr habt das Zünglein an der Wage,
> Das ich mit Sorge hielt im Gleichgewicht,
> Ihr habt es rohen Drängens angestoßen,
> Es schwankt, und blut'ge Todeslose fallen
> Aus beiden Schalen auf die bange Welt. (ll. 1419–23)

Then he is told that Mathias is challenging his authority in Bohemia and marching on Prague. Grillparzer has here fused into one incident details from Mathias' two attacks on the city (of 1608 and 1611). The "Majestätsbrief" of 1609, in which Rudolf undertook to recognize protestantism in Bohemia, is also introduced here as the price which the Bohemian nobles exact for supporting him against Mathias. When the nobles are announced, Rudolf is seized with the desire to assert his authority, as is underlined when he shouts for his sword. But he checks this aggressive display and tells Julius to put the sword aside. Having granted the nobles their charter, he demands their support against Mathias, and lapses into his former aggressiveness (ll. 1661–2). But distant cannon fire—a concrete representation of civil war—brings him to submit rather than unleash the misery of war. He knows how near he has come to betraying his ethic of "Nicht ich, nur Gott":

> In diesen Adern sträubt sich noch der Herrscher
> Und Zorn und Rachsucht glüht in meiner Brust. (ll. 1704–5)

His irascibility has been clear from the first and it is because he feels he is the prey of his passions that he shows so much diffidence.

At the very moment when he seems to have calmed himself and determined to sacrifice his personal interests by avoiding war, Leopold arrives and tempts him to revenge against Mathias by offering him the army he has recruited in Passau. In a brief monologue (the first in the play) Julius voices the anxiety of this crucial moment:

> O, daß nun nicht der Groll, gekränkte Würde,
> Und die Empfindung, die, wenn aufgeregt,
> Gern übergeht in jegliches Empfinden:
> Von hart zu weich, von Innigkeit zu Zorn,
> Ihn hinreißt einzuwill'gen in das Schlimmste:
> Zu handeln, da's zu spät. (ll. 1743–8)

The appropriate action at the appropriate time would have been to remove Klesel from the scene before he could lead Mathias into rebellion. Then Klesel himself enters, bringing Mathias' terms, and if war is to be avoided Rudolf must submit to the humiliation of dealing with this man he has most cause to hate. It is more than he can bear, and he is so angered that he gives Leopold what he had come for, namely written permission to bring his army to Bohemia. He immediately repents this action, but nothing can now stop the intemperate Leopold from invading Bohemia, and the arrival of his army before Prague can only make its citizens turn against the Emperor who had called in these foreign troops. And so by the beginning of Act IV Rudolf is virtually a prisoner of the people of the city.

Grillparzer noted while planning the play: "Am Schluß des III Aktes soll der Kaiser endlich *handeln* und dadurch sich noch tiefer ins Unglück stürzen" (I, 21, 141). By calling in Leopold's army he has taken decisive political action, not from insight (which still counsels him to inaction) but from the worst in his character—the anger and resentment of which we saw him capable in Act I. The introduction of Klesel to provoke his rage at the end of Act III is unhistorical. In history Rudolf was all too ready to proceed against Mathias or indeed anyone who interfered with his authority (Stieve writes of his "Größenwahn" and "krankhafte Rachgier"). But Grillparzer's Rudolf retains our sympathy since we see the strongest provocation is necessary before anger can obscure his judgement here.

During the upheaval while Prague is under fire, Don Cäsar frees himself from the arrest under which Rudolf has kept him since his return from Hungary, and makes his way to Lukrezia's house. At several points the epithet "wildverworren", so often applied to the times, is predicated of him, showing that his lack of self-control is symbolical of the turbulent age. His instability is nowhere more apparent than in the second scene of Act IV, when he goes to Lukrezia fully convinced that he only wants to talk quietly with her, but in fact, after a short conversation, murders her. This quality of his character has been apparent from the first scene of the play, where he abandoned his violent defence of Russworm as soon as Lukrezia appeared, and, after her departure, felt obliged to apologize to him for having allowed himself to be distracted. It was Lessing who said that a dramatist must plan a character's actions "Nach Massgebung des einmal angenommenen Charakters", and in this play Grillparzer shows the salient characteristics (so important for the later action) of Cäsar, Mathias, Ferdinand, Rudolf and Klesel as early as the first Act.

Cäsar is recaptured at the end of this scene. Leopold, we are told, has been driven off, and order restored in the city. When Rudolf next appears his loss of power is made clear by pantomime. He refuses to let Julius kiss his hand, allowing him only to shake it and thereby making it clear that he now regards Julius as an equal, not a subject. His behaviour here is exactly as it was when he first appeared in Act I, in that the audience and the other characters are left to infer his thoughts from his gestures, for he speaks not a word until a servant comes and demands the key of Cäsar's cell from Julius. Cäsar is bleeding to death, yet Rudolf refuses to let Julius give the key away, but takes it himself and throws it into a well, saying: "Er ist gerichtet, von mir, von seinem"—then he pauses and adds "Herrn" where he obviously intended in the first place to say "Vater". By suppressing this term in favour of the impersonal "Herr" he is surely not (as Kaderschafka supposes, see I, 6, 440 and 503) trying to avoid directing attention to irregularities in his own private life (he is represented as unmarried), but rather following his ethic of impersonal devotion to principle. It is true that throughout the play he has avoided calling Cäsar his son, and in Act I was furious when the latter intimated that he knew the truth. My point is that at this juncture in Act IV Rudolf finds it most difficult to suppress the word "Vater", and only succeeds because he is determined to make clear that his judgement of Cäsar is as impartial as his judgement of Russworm has been. Nor is it an act of sudden passion. The words he spoke to Prokop (ll. 1365–7) show that he is here acting in accordance with a preconceived principle.

There is, then, no contradiction between Rudolf's forbearance towards his brothers and his severe treatment of his son. Their misdeeds have been political, while his have concerned his private life, and from the beginning Rudolf has punished the immorality and selfishness of the individual, but failed to deal effectively with that of the group, the sect, the class. So close is the correspondence of his behaviour in this scene, where he condemns Cäsar, with his conduct in Act I that here, as there, he does not speak a single coherent sentence to anyone until his attention is drawn to the private misdeeds committed by individuals, and in both cases he speaks to pass sentence of death. Julius expressly draws attention to this disparity in the ways in which he deals on the one hand with private and on the other with public vice:

> O, daß er doch mit gleicher Festigkeit
> Das Unrecht ausgetilgt in seinem Staat,
> Als er es austilgt nun in seinem Hause.   (ll. 2193–5)

It was surely to emphasize this disparity that Grillparzer deviated from some historical facts concerning Russworm. The historical Russworm did not commit a "feiger Mord" nor was he condemned by Rudolf. According to Grillparzer's source, quoted in the standard edition of the play, "der Kayser hat ihm den Pardon gegeben, der ist aller aus Practiken verhalten und die Execution entzwischen vorgenommen worden, und hat der Kayser solche Übereilung hoch beklagt" (I, 6, 420). Grillparzer has made changes here in order to portray Rudolf's capacity for resolute action.

Nearly all critics of this play have either denied Rudolf's unity of character, and asserted that his firm measures against his general and his son are not to be reconciled with his political inactivity and his readiness to forgive his brothers: or else they have regarded the condemnation of Russworm and Cäsar as trifling episodes which can be ignored or explained away by special pleading.* This latter view entails regarding all the scenes involving Don Cäsar and Lukrezia as unimportant and ill-connected with the rest. Lukrezia (the only woman in the dramatis personae) is indeed a colourless character of no interest in her own right, but this surely suggests that Grillparzer saw her function to lie elsewhere. And that Cäsar is allotted no inconsiderable part and yet does not influence the political situation suggests that he too is important for another reason. Furthermore, to regard the Russworm episode as a trifle fails to explain why Grillparzer here deliberately deviated from the historical facts.

The failure of critics to appreciate the significance of Rudolf's behaviour to Cäsar and Russworm is probably due to their assumption that Grillparzer's Rudolf is meant to illustrate the familiar generalization that reflection often inhibits action: that if a man's intellectual processes are complex and protracted they will absorb much of his total energy, and that for this reason we commonly find greater energy in action from men in whom these processes are brief and limited. It is to this generalization that Ranke appeals in his account of the historical Rudolf:

> Während Rudolf den kosmischen Gesetzen und dem Zusammenhang der himmlischen und irdischen Dinge nachforschte, waren ihm die Zügel des Reichs, die ihm anvertraut waren, entschlüpft.
> Denn beides—ausgebreitete Wissenschaft und energisches Handeln —ist selten dem Menschen zugleich verliehen.

But Grillparzer has deliberately deviated from the motives ascribed to the historical Rudolf in order to bring out a different interpretation of his character.

By the end of Act IV Ferdinand and Max have reached Prague to mediate between Rudolf and Mathias. But Rudolf realizes that compromise will be unstable and that the head of state must be in a strong enough position to command the respect of agitators and

*I have given references to some of the critics I have in mind in ref. 52, p. 172.

give them pause (ll. 2324–5, cf. ll. 1169–71). And as Mathias already controls Hungary and Austria, Rudolf determines to yield the crown of Bohemia to him. Although Rudolf remains emperor, all effective power is now with his brother, and the bitterness of his experiences has brought him close to death.

The final Act takes us to Mathias in Vienna. Its function is to vindicate Rudolf by showing how catastrophe ensues when his policy is abandoned. The extremists on both sides, Ferdinand and Thurn, destroy the equilibrium that he had preserved and make war inevitable. What were almost Rudolf's last coherent words had been an injunction of restraint to Ferdinand:

> Was dir als Höchstes gilt: die Überzeugung,
> Acht sie in Andern auch, sie ist von Gott.   (ll. 2353–4)

But Ferdinand has been chosen to follow Mathias as King of Bohemia (ll. 2580–2) and is determined to stamp out the Protestant faith there as he had done in his own Styria. For their part, the Bohemian Protestants insist that they be granted all the concessions wrested from Rudolf in the "Majestätsbrief". And Thurn has expressed their defiance by throwing the Catholic regents from the window of the palace at Prague. Thurn's "Lust an Unruh" was well known to Rudolf (l. 1512), and once his restraining hand has been withdrawn both Thurn and Ferdinand are free to precipitate a conflict, each confident that his own side can win. There is thus now open rebellion in Bohemia, and Ferdinand is able to show Mathias that he can only quell it with the aid of the Catholic powers (the Pope, Spain and Bavaria) whose influence Rudolf had steadfastly resisted (ll. 1556–62) because he knew that it would mean persecution and war. Furthermore, the Catholic powers are prepared to support the two archdukes only on condition that Klesel (who inspired the policy of tolerating Protestants whereby Mathias climbed to power) be removed from office. And so Mathias has to allow Klesel to be taken from him. Once again he has been outmanoeuvred, as before in the Netherlands—in Act I Grillparzer alluded to his attempt to secure power there in 1577—and in battle with the Turks. He thus survives to contemplate a situation he cannot control. As he depended on Klesel, so will Ferdinand become the creature of Wallenstein. Klesel's prediction to this effect (ll. 2694–701) is confirmed when we learn that Wallenstein has already acted without consulting his master. He is even blinder to the dangers of a conflagration than is Ferdinand, and jubilantly declares:

> Der Krieg ist gut, und währt' er dreißig Jahr.   (l. 2851)

In this final Act Grillparzer represents Rudolf's death (1612), Ferdinand's nomination to follow Mathias as King of Bohemia (1617), Klesel's removal from office (1618) and the "Prager Fenstersturz" which opened the Thirty Years' War (1618) as all occurring in the same year. And his purpose was not merely to concentrate the action, but to represent the war as an immediate consequence of abandoning Rudolf's policy. When Duke Julius announces his master's death he is able to defend his inaction with the simple observation:

> Wo nichts zu wirken, ist auch nicht zu handeln.   (ll. 2827)

Rudolf's tragedy lies where Grillparzer saw Hamlet's to lie, namely in "die Schwermut, in die der Mensch gerät, wenn er durch *gerechte* Bedenklichkeiten am Handeln gehindert wird" (see below, p. 165).

CHAPTER 4

TWO POSTHUMOUS PLAYS

1. Die Jüdin von Toledo

Die Jüdin von Toledo is one of the three plays Grillparzer withheld from publication in his lifetime. It did not achieve a stage success until fifteen years after his death, when it was given in Berlin.[54, p. 88] Even today it has received comparatively little attention, perhaps because it is in some ways unlike his other plays. One can hardly call it a historical tragedy in the sense in which *König Ottokar* and *Ein Bruderzwist*, packed with historical detail, deserve the name. It is historical fact that the hero of the play, Alfonso VIII of Castile, was defeated by the Moors at the battle of Alarcos in 1195. Poets and historians tried to explain this humiliation by linking it with his love for a beautiful Jewess, so that his defeat could appear as a just punishment for his betrayal of his faith.* The whole story of his love for this girl seems to be a good example of the process whereby myths are made; it is absent from the oldest chronicles which describe his reign; there is an obvious motive for its concoction; and the warrior or hero who dallies with his mistress in neglect of his duties is a familiar mythological motif (Ulysses tarried with Calypso, Hercules with Omphale, Tannhäuser with Venus).† This play, then, is unlike those replete with historical detail, and the simplicity of its plot makes it much easier to follow. Like Grillparzer's Greek plays, it

*See p. xv of the editor's introduction to the play in I, 7.
†Wurzbach[54, p. 86] gives these and also some Spanish examples. He nevertheless thinks that the story of Alfons' love has a "historischer Kern", although he stresses that none of the details associated with it in the extant narratives can be true (*ibid.*, pp. 89, 93).

depicts the first awakening of love, and also shares their tendency to concentrate the action by constructing a simple plot, minimizing changes of scene, and making the total time-span short. Outer action is, however, more important than in *Sappho* or *Des Meeres und der Liebe Wellen*, but less so than in *Ein treuer Diener*.

Initially the king is thinking only of his duty—to lead his people against the Moors. His character is in every way unblemished ("fleckenlos", as Manrique says). But he is also completely untried. He has had no experience of women, and only became aware of their existence when the prim, colourless Leonore was led to him as his bride. When he admits that he could love her more warmly if she were less perfect, she looks so horrified that he has to cancel this disclosure of his inmost feelings and pass it off as a joke (ll. 182–7). How well we understand that he can feel nothing warmer than respect for this severe (the epithet is his) woman, who remains coldly indifferent to his attempts to please and delight her (ll. 200–2) and, when pressed, thanks him without enthusiasm (l. 216). One can imagine too the marriage he has had with a wife who regards the sexual connection as "ein Greuel jedem Wohlgeschaffenen", as something intrinsically loathsome which is elevated by marriage into a solemn duty (ll. 1202–5). The exaggerated prudery of the court ladies makes him cry, despairingly "O Sittsamkeit/Noch sittlicher als Sitte!" (such word-play is common in this text). Altogether the decorum of court behaviour is for him, not merely boring (l. 347) but even stifling (l. 621). Then he is confronted with a beautiful, vivacious girl who, because she has absolutely nothing to commend her but her lively attractiveness, can only stimulate him sexually, and that to the highest degree. She seems like a breath of fresh air after the stiltedness to which the court has accustomed him (ll. 725–30), and he is completely captivated. In Act V, in an extended simile very typical of Grillparzer's style, the king compares her effect on him with that of the oasis on the desert traveller (ll. 1691–8).

His companion Garceran stands to him much as Hero's uncle to her; from his more experienced view he can see the danger while the king is still completely oblivious of it (ll. 556–7). Garceran is no debauchee (the king says he is "wacker, ob gleich jung und rasch"), but has known enough philandering to see that it is the king's very inexperience that makes him a helpless prey to the girl's charms:

> O, daß doch dieser König seine Jugend,
> Der Knabenjahre hast'gen Ungestüm
> In Spiel und Tand, wie mancher sonst, verlebt!
> Allein als Kind von Männern nur umgeben,
> Von Männern großgezogen und gepflegt,
> Genährt vorzeitig mit der Weisheit Früchten,
> Selbst seine Ehe treibend als Geschäft,
> Kommt ihm zum erstenmal das Weib entgegen,
> Das Weib als solches, nichts als ihr Geschlecht
> Und rächt die Torheit an der Weisheit Zögling.
>
> (ll. 851–60)

Again we see that, if the hero's experience had been different, there would have been no tragedy. It is not that he is congenitally endowed with tendencies that will lead him inevitably to disaster, but that his circumstances are such as to make him the helpless victim of certain emotions, which, in other circumstances, might well never have been aroused at all, or have been stimulated without disastrous consequences. If he had sown his wild oats as a young man, he would now shrug his shoulders at the Jewess, knowing that a woman who can offer him nothing but sex, and whose character he cannot respect, could give him no permanent satisfaction. But as things are, he is the helpless victim of his passion for long enough to neglect urgent business of state and alienate his people. When he comes to his senses again in Act IV, he diagnoses his own case as that of the basically good man who has gone astray, and makes it clear (in the spirit of Grillparzer's theory of tragedy) that it could have happened to the best of men. He tells his queen:

> Du fühlst dann, daß Verzeihen Menschenpflicht
> Und niemand sicher ist, auch nicht der Beste. (ll. 1416–17)

No one lays villainous snares in this play. The Jewess initially wants merely to impress the king, to be noticed by him. Like many young and good-looking women, she is very conscious of her beauty and of the way she is envied for it, and enjoys being found attractive. She is not bent on seduction, but wants to make her power felt by compelling attention. This desire for approval or will to power is a major determinant of human behaviour, and power over others is itself pleasurable, being associated with strength and success, while to lack it is to feel an abject, slavish dependence. The will to power is, in many of its manifestations, an instinctive tendency and does not imply conscious strategy, of which Rahel is certainly incapable. She does everything on impulse; that is why her behaviour seems so contradictory, as one impulse succeeds another. Thus her initial confidence and even defiance collapses once she feels in danger (we are told how easily she is frightened, 1. 608), only to reappear at once as soon as she sees that the danger is passed (ll. 528–30). In her terror she clings to the king's feet, laying her head upon his knees. The queen retires in disgust at this apparent display of sensuality and at her husband's toleration of it. He, not knowing that male and female behaviour are complementary, that the helplessness of the female stimulates the male to be strong and protective, is amazed to find this happening in the present case; that the female is "stark" (exerts her most powerful influence) when she is "schwach":

> . . . Im Grunde wunderlich,
> Ein feiger Mann er wird mit Recht verachtet
> Und dies Geschlecht ist stark erst, wenn es schwach.
>
> (ll. 388–90)

Rahel is not an adventuress but a child, a spoiled child used to having its every impulse gratified. As soon as she no longer feels in danger, she begins to play and delight in the fancy dresses she has discovered (Garceran's contempt for her superficiality is well brought out when in his report of this incident he repeatedly refers to her with the impersonal "man"—ll. 430–8). Fine clothes, in which she can display herself to advantage, are what interest her (ll. 563, 45–50). The king more than once calls her "Kind" (ll. 609, 899), and Esther explains her treatment of the king's picture by saying:

> Sie ist nur ein verwöhnt, verwildert Mädchen
>
> . . . . .
>
> Es kam ihr ein, und also tat sie's eben.   (ll. 634–6)

Because she does everything on impulse she is, as the king comes to realize, a "Törin, die sich zehnmal/In jedem Atemzuge widerspricht" (ll. 1062–3). But this capriciousness suits her ("es steht ihr wohl", as he says, l. 901) and continues to fascinate him to the point of helplessness. He says in retrospect:

> All, was sie tat, ging aus aus ihrem Selbst,
> Urplötzlich, unverhofft und ohne Beispiel.   (ll. 1686–7)

The nobles who have her murdered act from the highest motives. The opening scene of Act IV makes it clear that only the death of Rahel will release the king from his bondage. If she is left alive, he will return to her and place the nation in jeopardy as before (ll. 1179–80). The queen who counsels' her murder to clear herself from the stigma of concubinage (ll. 1211–13) is to a certain extent redeemed by wavering when this dreadful resolve has to be translated into action (ll. 1769–71). The nobles realize that their murder of the girl was an act of insurrection; they were "Das Gute wollend, aber nicht das Recht" (l. 1761). All alike are guilty without villainy, and Esther's words which conclude the play voice recognition of this:

> Dann seid Ihr schuldig, auch, und ich—und sie.
> Wir stehn gleich jenen in der Sünder Reihe;
> Verzeihn wir denn, damit uns Gott verzeihe.

In this play Grillparzer takes his usual care to avoid making his characters behave in an unlifelike, implausible way in order to reveal their natures. The initial situation and the characters of the two girls and of their father are conveyed by means of an argument. This is always an effective method of exposition, for it is made to seem that the characters' prime concern is not with the audience, but with their own point of view, and it is in quite naturally arguing their own convictions that they give the necessary information. The subject of the argument (whether to stay in the park) tells us of the inferior position of the Jews in this society; Rahel's exuberance and determination to stay and impress the king draws her character as much as does Esther's contrasting silence. And the difference in character between the two girls is at the same time underlined by Isaak's story of their very different mothers.

Isaak is a caricature of a Jew, pompously self-righteous, larding his discourse with Old Testament allusions, and with a constant eye on his pocket. His way of commenting on Rahel's fine clothes and shoes is to say that every step she walks costs a threepenny piece. An astute merchant, he is not taken in by the fancy-dress crown, but recognizes it as

> . . . nicht Gold, vergüldet Blech,
> Man kennt es am Gewicht, gilt zwanzig Heller . . . (ll. 540–1)

That he even gives it a price in this parenthesis is a touch which makes us smile contemptuously. He is in fact a comic character of a kind not infrequent in Grillparzer's later plays (e.g. Hero's father, and Libussa's three suitors. Even Bancbanus has such comic traits.) It is his early tragedies (including *Das goldene Vließ*) that are completely lacking in comic elements. It seems that he outgrew his dependence on the unrelieved austerity of Weimar classicism.

The difference in character between Isaak and his daughter Esther is finely brought out by their different reactions to Alfons' inquiry as to where in the town they live. The father senses an advantage to be gained by enticing the king, and so he quickly gives the address. Esther, quietly resigned to injustice and suffering, and more far-seeing than any of her family, envisages the possibility of their eviction (ll. 614–16). Esther is Grillparzer's spokesman for his own perspicacious pessimism. Of this, the words with which she concludes the play form the best example.

The drawing of the king's character begins with the marked change in the quality of the dialogue on his entry. Up to that

point, we have had excited talk, in four-foot trochees, expressing
strong emotions (Isaak's fear, Rahel's exuberance). But this
vivacity is quite alien to the calm, passionless manner of life of
the king, and so when the Jewish family runs off, and the king and
his attendants enter, there is a change to longer lines (five-foot
iambs) and to longer speeches. Back here in Toledo the king is
naturally reminded of his early life, and narrates it to his queen
at some length. Grillparzer had employed the same type of
contrast in quality of dialogue for the same purpose (to bring out
differences of character) at the beginning of *König Ottokar*. That
play too begins with excited talk, prompted there by anxiety and
anger. But when Margareta enters, the dialogue conveys a much
more even emotion—her grief—and the fragmentation gives way
to long speeches as she relates the story of her woes and expresses
her joyless resignation in her lot. Alfons' equanimity is of a different kind; it is not the fruit of disappointment but the result of
never having experienced the bright things of life:

> Das Aug gekehrt auf eines Gegners Dräun,
> Blieb mir kein Blick für dieses Lebens Güter.   (ll. 179–80)

This narrative of the king's early life is a good example of how
Grillparzer adapted his sources to advantage. In Lope de Vega's
Judia de Toledo the king's boyhood is enacted and occupies the
whole of the first Act. Since the rest of the play concerns experiences much later in his life, there is something of a hiatus.*
Grillparzer avoided this by his brief narration which tells us not
only the king's past, but also his character and the influences which
formed it.

Grillparzer normally avoids narrative as a means of revealing
character and prefers direct action, for the obvious reason that it
is more realistic. In real life people do not tell us what their
character is and how it has been formed by their experience. We
have to infer it from such of their behaviour as comes to our
notice, and so plays which require this of us will tend to seem
lifelike. He also leaves a great deal to his actors. As Scherer has

---

*For detailed comparison of the two plays see ref. 13, pp. 143 ff.

said, the actor who plays Grillparzer "hat mehr zu ergänzen, als bei einem declamationssüchtigen, redeseligen Dramatiker". [42, p. 217] But those who read his plays instead of seeing them performed must supply the necessary "Ergänzung" for themselves, and the task is often beyond English readers, who sometimes suppose, for instance, that Zawisch is helplessly in love with Kunigunde, that Rahel is a calculating huntress, and so on. Even German commentators are not incapable of this kind of misunderstanding. L. Hradek, the editor of *Die Jüdin* in Sauer's edition of Grillparzer's works, takes Alfons' sharp words to Isaak (l. 521) as indicative of his contempt for the Jews (I, 7, 188). In actual fact he does not share the contemptuous attitude of his grandees (typified by Manrique, ll. 392-5), and even Garceran, ll. 480-1, but has defended the Jews (ll. 288-90) and, just before the incident to which Hradek refers, has spoken of them at length in terms which Garceran describes as "gespendet Lob" (l. 514). His impatient "Zur Sache, Was Geschwätz" to Isaak indicates not contempt but jealousy, for Isaak has just said that Rahel loves Garceran. It is only if we perceive the king's growing jealousy that we can realize how strong his interest in Rahel is becoming. The first indication is when he warns Garceran not to take liberties with her as he escorts her away. When she then declares that she is too exhausted to walk unsupported, he rebukes Garceran for immediately offering her his arm, and thinks it better for his sister to support her. He then sends a messenger to report on Garceran's behaviour as an escort, but cannot wait and comes to investigate himself. It is then that his jealousy flares up in the incident to which Hradek refers. A final indication of his jealousy is given when he cannot bear the thought of leaving Rahel's picture in another's possession: "Doch wär' es dort erwärmt von fremder Wärme." It is very much in accordance with Grillparzer's technique to reveal thoughts and feelings in this indirect way. Scherer says, appositely, that in his plays "Wir bekommen nicht lange Monologe zu hören mit 'soll ich—oder soll ich nicht'. Wir sehen, wie die Entscheidung fällt, und es ist uns genug Material an die Hand gegeben, um zu beurtheilen, warum sie so und nicht anders erfolgen mußte."[42, p. 235] An example is Alfons' decision at the end of Act II to take the girl to his remote castle of Retiro. The only two monologues he has in this Act (both short) express his determination *not* to succumb to temptation.

After he has met the Jewess, he is puzzled by his own confusion. Both this confusion and his bewilderment at it are brought out by his harping on the word "wirr".* He tries to banish from his mind the "wirre Bilder" she has evoked, but continues to see things "im wirren Licht" and sadly designates himself "die wirre Majestät". How completely his confusion deflects him from the urgent political situation (which is constantly kept before our minds because so much that is decisive in the action, e.g. the nobles' revolt, depends on the danger from the Moors) is shown with almost comic effect when, with his eyes fixed on Rahel, he misunderstands what Garceran is trying to tell him:

Garceran.
                    Wenn's genehm,
   Kehr' ich zurück ins Lager, zu dem Heer.
König.
   Das Heer verließ das Lager? Und warum?

This is from Act III, and by this time, although she still fascinates him, he has been with her long enough to be conscious of her limitations, and so reacts impatiently to her whims. When, for instance, she complains that the path is too rough, he calls gruffly to his servants: "Legt einen Teppich ihr und macht ein Ende" (l. 893). And when she claims to be exhausted and immediately afterwards throws cushions about, he comments, with gentle sarcasm: "Die Mattigkeit, zum Glück, läßt etwas nach" (l. 898). Alfons' conflict between passion and duty is Grillparzer's invention. In Lope de Vega's play the king simply forgets his wife and kingdom and devotes himself entirely to the Jewess. Grillparzer, however, not only wished to write a psychological drama, but also to express the workings of his characters' minds without long monologues. And so in Acts III and IV, as in Act II, the king's

*I owe this point to Blackall.[6]

conflict between passion and duty is shown when he decides to act dutifully, but is nevertheless unable to carry this decision out. When he first appears in Act III he assures Garceran that he will put Rahel completely from his mind—not at once, but in a few days' time. Then she flirts with Garceran in a way that would have provoked the king to violent jealousy had it occurred earlier. Here he is not totally indifferent, but his greater independence of the Jewess is shown by the fact that it disgusts rather than enrages him, makes him more than ever conscious of her worthlessness, and brings him to decide to leave her at once and go to his army where he is needed. He sends his servant to fetch his armour, and she plays with the shield—she cannot even see the poor reflection of herself in it without vain thoughts (l. 1015). And her game with the helmet very nearly breaks his resolution to leave, so that he calls her "Du albern-spielend, töricht-weises Kind" (l. 1029)—wise because she knows how to deflect him from his purpose and retain her hold over him. But then Esther enters with news that compels him to leave. The nobles have revolted and unless he goes at once to dissolve their assembly, he will never regain his authority. Before his arrival at the council-chamber, the queen and nobles agree that they must ask him to order Rahel's execution and take the law into their own hands if he refuses. There follows the interview between the king and queen. He enters determined to put the past aside and act as a worthy monarch once more, and expresses his repentance in long speeches. She says little, and nothing at all of the plan to murder Rahel. But he knows (from what Esther has told him in Act III) what is afoot, and bursts into indignant condemnation of this resolve. As he looks at Rahel's picture, the fascination she still has for him reasserts itself (rekindled in part by the contrast with his wife's icy virtue). His penitence gives way entirely to anger, and he begins to chide his queen not only for her designs against Rahel but also for her alliance with the nobles. Then Don Manrique appears in the background, visible to her but not to him. She points to her husband and wrings her hands despairingly—gestures which tell Manrique that she has failed to persuade the king to agree to

Rahel's death. Manrique leaves, and as the king goes on venting his anger, she too withdraws quietly, and he tries to follow her to her room. When Manrique and Garceran enter, the two lines of dialogue they exchange make it clear that Manrique has determined to murder the Jewess without more ado, and that Garceran will, reluctantly, support him (ll. 1541–2). Garceran's help is necessary if the murderers are to enter the castle (ll. 1295–1301). Then, after they have left, the king returns, is told that the queen and all the nobles have left, and infers the truth.

I have tried to show that much of the action depends on the characters and that their ideas and emotions are conveyed clearly, yet not laboured. We are given sufficient to infer what they are thinking and feeling without resort to patently artificial devices. In some plays the characters are unconvincing not because they act implausibly but because they are so simplified that they show little more than one basic trait (e.g. jealousy, or hastiness of temper) on which the tragic outcome is made to depend. But in *Die Jüdin* they are both complicated and consistent. The inconsistencies of Rahel, Garceran and the king are only apparent. They, like real-life characters, are impelled to action not by one single motive; their actions represent the outcome of a conflict between different urges, and at different times now one, now another of these conflicting motives will be dominant and issue in behaviour that is apparently contradictory. Why, for instance, does Garceran first support the king and then betray him? It is because he feels strong loyalty to the king's person, and admiration for many of his qualities, but also sees that the interests of the community cannot be sacrificed to one individual. The king is able to appeal to the one motive and Garceran's father to the other. The latter motive is strengthened by his desire to avoid the taint of the king's dishonour, since he is anxious to wed the unblemished Dona Clara (who has no part to speak in the play, but who is introduced into Acts I and IV for the purpose of illuminating Garceran's character). Complex motivation, then, means apparent inconsistencies of behaviour, and Grillparzer thought that the best plays show precisely this: "Die Konsequenz der Leidenschaften ist das Höchste, was gewöhnliche Dramatiker schildern ... aber erst die aus der Natur gegriffenen Inkonsequenzen bringen Leben in das Bild und sind das Höchste der dramatischen Kunst" (II, 7, 352).

We have seen how often Grillparzer conveys ideas and emotions by means of visual devices as well as words. In his autobiography he even quotes "ut pictura poesis" to emphasize the importance of visual effects in drama (I, 16, 160). Thus, to express his conviction on the matter, he does not hesitate to use the phrase which Lessing's *Laokoon* had brought into disrepute. His plays appeal to the eye as well as the ear, and this combination represented, for him, the ideal. In his diary for 1817, he made a note of Cromwell's dashing down his watch as he stood before the Commons, and threatening that he would smash them as he did the watch. "Etwas Ähnliches", he commented, "müßte auf der Bühne von der herrlichsten Wirkung sein: so Wort und Bild zu gleicher Zeit!" (II, 7, 125).

Grillparzer's term for expressing states of mind by visible means is "Anschaulichkeit", and in 1820 he affirmed in his diary that "Es gibt für mich keinen andern Beweis als Anschaulichkeit" (II, 7, 295)—proof, that is, of a dramatist's capacity. It will not do to depict, say, a man's impetuosity by making him say he is impetuous, or even by making him use violent language. But if he betrays the trait by brandishing his sword at the slightest provocation as he speaks (as Don Cäsar does at the beginning of *Ein Bruderzwist*) then we have the ideal of "Wort und Bild zu gleicher Zeit".

The visible picture may be a gesture or an object handled. Rahel takes off an earring and pretends to throw it away. Isaak runs to recover it. Together with the accompanying words, her gesture conveys capriciousness, and his avarice (ll. 50–60). The stage directions which indicate Rahel's gestures in the latter part of Act I are particularly expressive. Her terror is brought out as she comes running in, kneels before the queen, and then tries to grasp her hands. But the queen turns her back on her (another effective gesture) and Rahel is again at a loss, until she notices the merciful eyes of the king. She flings herself down, "seinen Fuß umklammernd, das Haupt zu Boden gesenkt". When he orders her to rise, her strength fails her, and so she sits "den Ellenbogen aufs Knie und den Kopf in die Hand gestützt". When she does rise, her exhaustion is conveyed as she stands "in der Mitte der Bühne, mit gebrochenen Knien und gesenktem Haupte", and her sister has to straighten her dress at the neck—she cannot summon the strength herself.

There is a similar example in *Des Meeres und der Liebe Wellen*. Soon after Hero has admitted Leander to her tower, noises suggest that the guards outside are coming to look for the intruder. She hastily bids him hide, but the only room into which he can withdraw is her bedroom. When she is left alone, Grillparzer's directions express the shame, remorse and exhaustion she feels: "Sie senkt sich in den Stuhl, mit halbem Leibe sitzend, so daß das linke herabgesenkte Knie beinahe den Boden berührt, die Augen mit der Hand verhüllt, die Stirne gegen den Tisch gelehnt." And she proceeds to put these emotions into words, crying "O Scham und Schmach". Here, then, we have "Wort und Bild zu gleicher Zeit".

It was because Grillparzer wanted his plays to be acted and not merely read that he was careful to visualize what gestures he required from his actors, and to indicate them in such detail. He remarked to Foglar (30 December 1839) that "Der junge dramatische Dichter soll sich in das Parterre versetzen und zuschauen im Geiste, ob eine Person rechts oder links zu stehen kommt? ob sie die oder die Hand hebt oder senkt? sitzt oder steht? ja, sozusagen jeden Knopf am Kleide derselben sehen".[14, p. 3] This is certainly what he himself did in writing his own plays. His directions, however long, are not comments from the author which cannot be enacted. Whereas Hauptmann opens Act II of *Vor Sonnenaufgang* with stage directions which include the information that old Krause is the last guest to leave the inn *as always*, Grillparzer avoids including such items which can only be appreciated by a reader.

Another of his methods of using things the audience can see is to make a character address a part of the stage setting particularly relevant to the emotion he is feeling. Thus in Act IV of *Die Jüdin*, when the king is alone in the council-chamber, his attention is caught by the empty throne rising above the other chairs. The dialogue before his arrival stressed that this throne is his proper place, and he now prays that his conduct may reflect its dominating position, even when he is without the elevation which it imparts:

> Du hoher Sitz, die andern überragend,
> Gib', daß wir niedriger nicht sei'n als du,
> Auch, ohne jene Stufen, die du leihst,
> Das Maß einhalten des was groß und gut.   (ll. 1340–3)

Thus is his determination to resume his role of head of the realm expressed, and immediately afterwards he translates this decision into action by welcoming Eleonore as she comes to him. Another example occurs in Act V. Rahel is dead, and her murderers have left the rooms in disorder. Esther points to the jewellery lying scattered over the floor, and says to her father:

> Da liegen sie, die Trümmer unsres Glücks,
> Der bunte Tand, um dessentwillen wir,
> Ja wir, nur wir . . .
> Die Schwester opferten, dein töricht Kind.   (ll. 1751–4)

We had examples of the same technique in other plays (see above, p. 57), and many further instances could be given. For example, when Ottokar returns to his castle after his humiliation, he addresses its gate (visible on the stage) and expresses his sense of shame by saying he is too dishonoured to enter the castle, but must sit outside it as his own gatekeeper. Here again, his emotion is closely linked with something we can actually see, and by this means gains in vividness and immediacy. Another example is when Leander, who has been sitting with his back resting against a tree, jumps up, and expresses his determination not to leave Hero and return home by saying:

> Ich heim? Hier will ich wurzeln,
> Mit diesen Bäumen stehen Tag und Nacht
> Und immer schaun nach jenes Tempels Zinnen.   (ll. 801–3)

A fine example of "Anschaulichkeit" in *Die Jüdin* is the use Grillparzer makes of the two pictures. In the story as told by the French writer Cazotte, the girl's father put the king under a spell, which was effective only so long as she wore his picture and he hers. Grillparzer's technique as a dramatist is well illustrated by what he made of both the spell and the pictures. The former he deprived of its objective reality, since he wished to derive the king's behaviour from purely natural causes. Only Eleonore believes that a spell is involved and her belief in it is retained in order to bring out her prim character. She cannot understand on any other basis how Alfons acted as he did. And her phrase "ich fass' es nicht" (l. 1378) is not, with her, what it so often is, namely an attempt to draw attention to the superiority of the speaker, unaccompanied by any genuine effort to understand the party criticized. It is a real failure to understand the workings of passion, which to her are a closed book. When she tries to convince Alfons that he is bewitched, his reply underlines the derivation of the tragic outcome from natural causes, particularly his own character:

> Umgeben sind wir rings von Zaubereien,
> Allein wir selber sind die Zauberer
>
> .   .   .   .   .
>
> Und in der Welt voll offenbarer Wunder
> Sind wir das größte aller Wunder selbst.   (ll. 1429–34)

As for the pictures, Grillparzer has used them to express ideas and emotions. When, outside the "Gartenhaus", the king is told that Rahel, inside, is playfully caressing his picture.

> Nennt es Gemahl, spricht's an mit süßen Worten
> Und drückt's an ihre Brust.   (ll. 547–8)

his incipient passion is expressed by the gesture with which he reacts to this disclosure: "Der König geht mit starken Schritten auf das Gartenhaus zu." But he then checks himself and contrives to find (ll. 549–51) an apparently innocuous reason for going to her (as he also does later, l. 770). When he sees her playful behaviour, he first orders her to return the picture to its frame, but gives in when she insists on keeping it. After the humiliating interruption when he has to hide from the queen in the adjacent room, he feels thoroughly ashamed at his whole behaviour, and his determination to reassert his royal dignity and authority is made clear by his renewal of the demand that the picture be replaced. Rahel pretends to comply, and his disappointment at her apparent readiness to do so shows how deeply she has attracted him, for it suggests to him that her previous determination to keep his picture was a sham and did not stand for any deep affection (ll. 734–41).

Instead of replacing the picture Rahel has substituted one of herself, which the king then wears on a chain round his neck. The way he handles it contributes much to our understanding of his mind when he tries to reconcile himself with Eleonore in Act IV. He first lays it on a table, "auf immer abgetan" (l. 1471); but he cannot keep away from this table, and the sight of the image again puts Rahel's beauty in the foreground of his mind and makes him feel fury towards the queen and nobles who would destroy such loveliness. It is not until he sees Rahel dead that he throws the picture away. Nothing then remains of the vivacity that enthralled him, and his throwing away the picture is not the breaking of a magic spell, but simply an outward and visible sign that all the attraction he felt for her is gone.

The play shows the author's usual concern to present direct action rather than narrative. In his draft of a letter to Müllner concerning *Sappho* he said that the difference between dramatic and lyric poetry is that, in the former, the opinions and emotions of the characters should appear only as the substratum of the action (III, 1, 98). He recognized that Greek tragedy did not fulfil this ideal because—so he argued—it had only recently broken away from the epic. In a diary note of 1834 he insisted that its predominance of description and narration over action is not to be imitated by modern dramatists (II, 9, 164). In *Die Jüdin* little that could be directly enacted is narrated. The king's early life, which formed his character, belongs to the past and so has to be put into a narrative. The Moors' preparations for war are also only reported; a scene which showed their military camp would be too loosely connected with the rest. But practically everything else we witness as it happens. A good example is the murder of Rahel. As the curtain rises on Act V we see a room where the furniture is overturned, and hear shouting and fighting outside. Then a voice cries: "Das Zeichen tönt! Zu Pferde." The information suffices to let us know that the murder has been done off-stage, and the attackers have been given a prearranged signal to withdraw.

The change which comes over the king when he sees Rahel's dead body is an interesting example of Grillparzer's technique of making his presentation as direct as possible. It would not do for us merely to be told that the sight of her corpse has broken the spell. On the other hand, little could be conveyed in a scene where he actually stood by her body, unless he were to voice his feelings in a long declamatory monologue of the type Grillparzer was clearly trying to avoid in this play. Grillparzer's solution is to make the king go to her disfigured body for the purpose of fanning his hatred for her murderers and steeling himself to revenge; to make these murderers assemble on the empty stage during his absence, and to show the change that has come over him by portraying his utter inability to carry out, on his return, the revenge he intended, even though the murderers confront him, disarmed and helplessly awaiting his judgement. We are expecting him to return in a fury, but when he does re-enter he seems annihilated, and the great psychological change can then be shown in the ensuing dialogue.*

---

*Krispyn[24, pp. 405 ff.] agrees with the many critics who have held that the king's "sudden change of heart about Rahel" is not intelligible and mars the play. But I cannot see the difficulty. Rahel's hold on the king is exclusively sexual and, as he himself says, a corpse cannot fill his mind with "üppige Bilder", but leaves it free for the competing thoughts of "Weib und Kind und Volk" (ll. 1856-7). Krispyn, however, supposes that, for no adequate reason, the king is suddenly made an exponent of "the Kantian notion of virtue as the predominance of duty over inclination", so that the "final scenes . . . might be characterized as a Kantian tour de force".

Krispyn is led from curious premises to suspect a "basic flaw" of some kind in the play. They are: (1) "The royal garden at Toledo allegorizes the mythical Garden of Eden." (2) This "would seem to imply that Alphons and Rahel

I have already remarked that there are few monologues of any length in *Die Jüdin*. Grillparzer used the monologue much less profusely as he matured. In the early *Die Ahnfrau* Jaromir's monologue (one of many) in Act V continues for 250 lines. The other extreme is represented by *Ein Bruderzwist*, with only three short monologues in the whole play. That Grillparzer wrote fewer and shorter monologues is very much in keeping with his desire for action and visual effects, and to avoid speeches which would suit a reader but appear dull on the stage. What monologues he does include are often unobtrusively placed as an introduction to an Act. Thus Garceran introduces Act II by expressing his consciousness of how dangerous Rahel's character makes her to a man of probity, and Isaak begins Act V (after the noises-off indicating the murder) by creeping in half hidden under a carpet he drags along, and expressing his abject fear. Alternatively, the monologue may be equally unobtrusively spoken in a brief interval when the speaker is left alone. Rahel's antics with the carnival clothes alarm Esther; Rahel goes to fetch more finery to play with, leaving Esther alone for just long enough to voice her fears in a soliloquy of two lines (ll. 566–7). All the other monologues in this play are spoken by the king. In his first he is not alone; he is emerging from the room where he hid from the queen, and the eyes of all present are upon him. Here is a chance for a skilful actor to show in his face his sense of shame at the knowledge that his guilty retreat from his own wife has been witnessed by his courtiers. All keep a respectful distance as he expresses this emotion and also his determination to regain his reputation and authority (ll. 692–700). This resolve is then straightway shown in direct action, as he turns with some harshness on Garceran and reproaches him for what has happened.

This play also shows Grillparzer's usual concern to concentrate the action in time and place. Acts I, III, IV and V are unbroken in their action; only in Act II is there a change of scene within the Act. There is also only one break in the time sequence—between the end of Act II (when the king is about to begin his life with Rahel) and the beginning of Act III. This interval is indicated only indirectly—by the fact that Isaak has come to wield a position of power and influence, and by the king's impatience with Rahel and relative indifference to incidents which would have provoked his jealousy in Act II (see above, p. 135). The interval cannot be a long one. The Moors, who, we were told in Act I, are massing their armies, have still not launched an attack. This time interval is, of course, essential to the dramatic action, but Grillparzer avoids any direct statement that it has occurred (still less does he specify its length) in order to create the impression of an unbroken sequence. He said in his autobiography:

> Die Einheit der Zeit ist höchst wichtig. Die Form des Dramas ist die Gegenwart, welche es bekanntlich nicht gibt, sondern nur durch die ununterbrochene Folge des nach einander Vorgehenden gebildet wird. Die Nichtunterbrechung ist daher das wesentliche Merkmal derselben. (I, 16, 168.)

He said too that although imagination can bridge gaps in the time sequence, it is better for the dramatist not to require this of it. Unity of time thus "gibt der Handlung eine vorzügliche Stetigkeit und befördert das eigentliche Dramatische der Wirkung ungemein".* He means the effect of making the action appear to occur in the present. The impression of "eine Gegenwart" can only be created by a series of events which follow each other immediately, and if the unity of time is not kept, the drama is approximated to the epic, which narrates the past.

Another important reason Grillparzer gives for retaining the unity of time is that time itself influences motives and ideas. In *Die Jüdin* much depends on the way the king is repeatedly exposed to the stimulus of Rahel's company within a short period. After the initial meeting, he orders her to be taken away, but is told that "das Volk ist aufgeregt". So she must stay and he be exposed to constant sexual stimulation, until by the end of Act II it determines his actions entirely. Thus do "Empfindungen und Leidenschaften stärker werden durch die Zeit" (see above, p. 81).

---

*Quoted by Strich.[49, pp. 112-13]

2. Libussa

Libussa is not what one would have expected from Grillparzer and it is not surprising that, after its original production at the Burgtheater in 1874, it was not again given there for fifty years. [15, p. 238] Whereas his other plays are eminently stage-worthy, this one is fragmented by fourteen changes of scene. Even *König Ottokar* is broken up only in the final Act, where the battle scenes are loosely put together. Furthermore, *Libussa* abounds in monologues and even asides. Grillparzer uses both to an unusual extent to explain a situation, or the speaker's emotions and plans. A third way in which the play is unlike his others is that it gives riddles and philosophical disquisitions, and we ponder the meaning of what is said rather than feel strong emotion. Grillparzer was aware of this as a defect, and noted in 1831 that the play (which he was then writing) is "bloßes Gedankenzeug . . . beinahe ohne Gefühls-, wenigstens ohne Leidenschaftsmotive" (II, 9, 44–5).

Another factor which distinguishes the play is its characterization. That Libussa's two sisters are always seen together underlines the fact that they are not so much individuals as symbols or representatives of a contemplative mode of life which, for all its worth, is stamped by Grillparzer as a selfish one. Libussa's three suitors also always appear together and are not carefully drawn individuals. Other characters, such as the workmen and miners, are even more generalized. It is not Grillparzer's usual practice to have so many characters conceived only in general terms. That he does so here is particularly striking since the two principals are so carefully drawn. Primislaus, for instance, shows wisdom, courage, resourcefulness, altruism, and other traits in the various situations in which he is depicted.

Another element one does not associate with Grillparzer's later plays (after *Die Ahnfrau* and the spells and magic of *Das goldene Vließ*) is the supernatural. Libussa's mother was "eine göttergleiche Frau" and her children have supernatural powers. Kascha knows that Krokus has died and that Libussa was not with him at the time, before the news reaches her by natural means. That

Grillparzer retained such fairy-tale features from his sources means that in this play it would be inappropriate to seek meticulous motivation of details.

After Libussa's encounter with the peasant Primislaus she feels repelled by the life she has hitherto been leading with her sisters and longs for the warmth of a human relationship (ll. 402–4). Her curtness to him in the opening scene masks an affection which is less disguised in his absence, and it is because she now feels drawn to man and to human life that she agrees to accept the government of the country which her sisters have disdainfully declined. Tetka feels concern at her intention to abandon the contemplative life: "Wer handelt geht oft fehl", to which she replies: "auch wer betrachtet".

When the three noblemen woo her, she sets them a riddle. Giving them her golden chain (from which Primislaus has removed the jewel) she says:

> Wer mir die Kette teilt,
> Allein sie teilt mit Keinem dieser Erde,
> Vielmehr sie teilt, auf daß sie ganz erst werde;
> Hinzufügt was, indem man es verlor,
> Das Kleinod teurer machte denn zuvor:
> Er mag sich stellen zu Libussas Wahl,
> Vielleicht wird Er, doch nie ein Andrer ihr Gemahl.
>
> (ll. 670–6)

Although at this stage we can no more understand the riddle than they, it is hard to avoid laughing at them as they repeat the first lines of it in their bewilderment. Libussa summons a page-boy with a cushion, places the chain on it, and sends them off with him to solve the riddle. This comic picture is repeated in the next scene, when the lad leads them on to the stage again. Well may Domaslav say at this point: "Mir dünkt ich sehe Spott in seinen Augen." They meet Primislaus and ask his help, and as they repeat the riddle to him, his gestures (invisible to them) give the first indication of its meaning. As Lapak repeats the first two lines, Primislaus takes the chain, whose links are hooked together, and pulls it at both ends so that they are stretched apart. Thus "teilt", in the first line of the riddle means "separates", "parts", although the same word in the second line means "shares". At the word "Kleinod" Primislaus puts his hand upon his heart, where we know he keeps the jewel he took from Libussa's chain. He has realized that the third line means "pull the chain apart so as to insert the missing jewel and thus make the chain whole", as in fact he does in Act IV. He has also realized that the loss of the jewel has made it more valuable to Libussa because it has gone to the man she loves. In Act IV he recites this part of the riddle to her, and comments:

> O wüßtest du was mir bei diesem Wort
> Für Hoffnungen durch meine Seele stürmten!

Primislaus now knows that Libussa has chosen him to be her husband, and his first reaction is to go to her and claim her hand. But he lets his pride restrain him, and is angry that she should have run the risk that one of these nobles might have solved the riddle. As a recent critic has noted,[18, p. 457] his reasoning is not very cogent. Only he had sufficient information to reach a solution. It would have been more appropriate if his anger were here aroused because Libussa had left it to sheer chance whether the riddle should ever reach his ears. Both Libussa and Primislaus are reticent in expressing their feelings, and this frequently leads to misunderstandings in ways which ring very true to life. He decides not to go to her, but to let her know that he has heard and understood the riddle. For this purpose he deliberately misinterprets it to the three nobles, and himself gains possession of the chain, for which he exchanges the jewel.

When the nobles return to Libussa and report what has happened, she realizes that Primislaus has acted astutely, but is in turn angry with him for not coming to her. She determines to summon him to be the judge the nation needs. Her method of government was based on a much too idealistic view of human nature. Instead of trusting her with childlike faith, her subjects argue among themselves to establish their respective rights. To settle such disputes a firm hand is required—not Libussa's, who says "ich kann nicht hart sein" (l. 962). So she tells the nobles to take

Primislaus' horse, lead it to the point where she bade him leave her, and follow it as it finds its way to its stable.

Act III begins with a long monologue in which Primislaus expresses the conflict between his pride and his love for Libussa. He wishes she would come to him, riding the horse he had given her, and then he sees the horse with the nobles following it. Well may he ask "Bin ich im Land der Märchen und der Wunder?" (l. 1076). This is one of many fairy-tale elements which make this the least realistic of Grillparzer's plays. Meanwhile, Libussa, sick of the frustration of governing her all-too-human subjects, has sent her servant to ask her sisters to receive her back, and a whole scene is now devoted to philosophizing from the sisters. They refuse her request on the ground that she is now too embroiled in human affairs to resume the life of contemplation. They know— another fairy-tale motif—that the jewel of her chain has been in the hands of a man for whom she felt affection, because it no longer gleamed when it was returned (ll. 1157–62).

When Primislaus finally comes to her she is offended by his pride, tells him he cannot be judge in the land but may stay the night at the castle before returning to his farm. Her intention is to impress him with its splendour, and at the beginning of Act IV we see her servant Wlasta taking him on a tour of inspection. This fourth Act could well form part of a comedy. Libussa is curious as to what Primislaus will say to Wlasta, and so she disguises herself as the servant who stands holding the torch beside them. Wlasta's restlessness in the presence of this "servant" makes Primislaus suspect the truth. And so, addressing Wlasta, he both declares his love for Libussa and justifies his proud and reticent behaviour. Libussa betrays her growing excitement by trembling and waving the torch she holds.

Wlasta has put the jewel on a table and told Primislaus that Libussa wishes him to return the chain which belongs with it. But he is determined to acquire this jewel, and so flirts with Wlasta, making Libussa run off in indignation, and Wlasta too when she finds herself alone with him in the darkness. He is then able to pocket the jewel, and triumphantly declares "die List gelang".

But his joy is premature, for Libussa has him let down through a trap-door into the room below. Curme makes this episode even more comic by supposing that Primislaus is let down "into a cold bath below, which cools off his ardor a bit and affords Libussa a little revenge".* Now Primislaus does say, immediately after his fall:

> —Der Boden schwankt, die Sinne schwindeln.
> Aus steiler Höhe rasch herabgeglitten,
> Schlägt noch die Erde Wellen unter mir
> Und die Bewegung setzt sich fort ins Innre.

But the "Wellen" are not water-waves. He means that he still feels the earth reverberating after his heavy fall, and that the movement of the ground has communicated itself to his mind, so that he feels concussion and shock—not, as Curme supposes, "the cold chills from the cold water which are running over and through him". There is no mention of cold any more than of water! Grillparzer, of all people, would not write a tragedy which included a slapstick incident, and it is surprising that he went even as far as he did in the direction of comedy here. The departure from "high tragedy" in these scenes repelled him (even though it belonged to his plan) and deterred him from completing the play for many years (I, 20, 330).

The Act concludes with the announcement that Primislaus and Libussa will be man and wife. He sums up the cause of their misunderstandings:

> Wir waren wie die Kinder wenn sie schmollen,
> Wegweisend was der Wunsch zumeist begehrt. (ll. 1778–9)

The tragedy of the fifth Act comes as a surprise after this happy ending to the fourth, when there is no indication that tragedy will occur, nor why, and it is not surprising that there has been a lengthy debate as to the cause of the catastrophe.† What is stressed repeatedly in this final Act is the difference in outlook

---

*Ref. 10, p. lxxiii: cf. the note on p. 183, where he again says that he "has fallen into a body of cold water".

†Stein [46, pp. 155 ff.] summarizes the various views.

between the spouses. She values the talents of the individual, particularly the noblest ones which she designates as "Begeisterung und Glauben und Vertrauen" (l. 2391)—the inspiration of the leader and the trusting obedience of his subjects that is complementary to it. Her sisters value inspiration and communion with higher things so exclusively that they cut themselves off from the untalented, from "der Pöbelschwarm", in order to pursue their life of contemplation (ll. 1986–8). Libussa, in contrast, wishes not to turn her back on man, but to enrich his life with the noblest capacities of the most gifted individuals. She finds, however, that even the man she loves and respects most, is prepared to sacrifice what is most noble to the good of the many:

> Das Edle selbst, das wohltut höherm Sinn,
> Weist er zurück und duldet das Gemeine
> Wenn allgemein der Nutzen und die Frucht.   (ll. 1968–70)

For her, whatever exists has a right to do so, independently of the claims of others, while for him each must justify its distinctive character and privileges by showing that they contribute to the good of the whole:

> All was sich selbst gemacht im Lauf der Dinge
> Dünkt als natürlich mir zugleich im Recht.
> Mein Gatte aber prüft und untersucht
> Und jeder Anspruch muß ihm Rede stehn
> Als Allen nützlich in der Hand des Einen.   (ll. 1995–9)

She hates the processes which bring the talented to the level of the ungifted, and for this reason she opposes his plan to build a city where man will no longer live as an individual, but where

> Die enge Nähe, störende Gemeinschaft
> Schleift ab das Siegel jeder eignen Geltung.   (ll. 2031–2)

He, for his part, does not wish to exclude or ignore the individual gifted with rare or even supernatural powers, but to harness them for the good of the whole. To this end he begs Libussa, in her capacity as priestess and prophetess, to bless the site they have chosen for the town which they will name Prague. She at first

demurs, since she is both physically weak after a recent confine-
ment, and also no longer used to exercising her powers of prophecy. Since she left her sisters she has not practised these gifts,
and both she and Wlasta fear that the strain of resuming them
will be too much for her. Wlasta warns her:

> Du hast vermengt dich mit dem Irdischen,
> Bist ausgetreten aus dem Kreis der Deinen.
> Die Steigerung, die heilige Begeistrung,
> Dir sonst natürlich, ist nur noch ertrozt,
> Erzwungen. Wags nicht, du erträgst es nicht.   (ll. 2269–73)

But just as Primislaus values the supernatural powers of inspiration
that she represents, so she accepts his standpoint to the extent of
wishing to contribute to the common good:

> Ich will nicht nutzlos sein im Kreis der Dinge.
> Kann ich nicht wirken in der Zeit, die neu,
> So will ich segnen.   (ll. 2274–6)

Her prophecy is, however, more of a sombre indictment than a
blessing. She begins it by deploring their decision to live collec-
tively:

> Und eine Stadt gedenkt ihr hier zu baun;
>
> .   .   .   .   .
>
> Nicht Ganze mehr, nur Teile wollt ihr sein.   (ll. 2328–32)

In a town they will necessarily abandon the life where each
individual is "ein Wesen das er selbst und sich genug" (l. 2331).
She says too that when men live together their talk of universal
love will not be an emotion, like love of family or neighbour, but
an idea, or even a mere empty catch-word—a formula for the sake
of which men will persecute and kill:

> Was du Empfindung wähnst ist nur Gedanke,
> Und der Gedanke schrumpft dir ein zum Wort,
> Und um des Wortes willen wirst du hassen.   (ll. 2361–3)

Worse will follow when the sword is replaced by cunning, and not
the warrior but the intriguer rules the world (ll. 2383–6). She
naturally feels that there is no place for her in the present, nor in

the future that she sees here. Her vision does indeed show a remote future in which what she values will again be esteemed. When man is sated with material comfort and has extended his control over nature to its utmost limits, then:

> Wird er die Leere fühlen seines Innern.
>
> . . . . .
>
> Dann kommt die Zeit, die jetzt vorübergeht,
> Die Zeit der Seher wieder und Begabten. (ll. 2474–83)

But this solace is centuries distant. She dies at the end of this prophetic speech, dispirited because mankind, which she loves, has no place for her and her values, and exhausted at the efforts she has made, in her physical weakness, to read the future. As Grillparzer noted, in a plan of 1822: "Weissagend von einem kommenden ehernen Zeitalter, schaudernd vor dem was sie sieht, erliegt ihre gebrochene Natur, sie stirbt" (I, 20, 386). Her sisters can survive because they cut themselves off from man, while she cannot. Kascha asks her at the end: "Warum hast du an Menschen dich geknüpft?" She replies: "Ich liebe sie", and she affirms this love even though Kascha warns her: "Sie aber töten dich." If Grillparzer had presented the two sisters more sympathetically, it would be possible to say (with many critics) that Libussa's tragedy is due to her abandonment of the contemplative life. Such a view would accord with the account of Grillparzer's conception of tragedy given by Staiger and Papst (see below, p. 159)—that action leads to disaster, and that the dramatist sets up detached contemplation as an ideal. But surely Libussa's love of man, which prompts her to active participation in his affairs, is not something we would have her renounce, so as to become like her ungracious sisters. And Papst admits that in this play "the realm of *Sammlung*" —the detached contemplation which, he says, normally represents Grillparzer's ideal—has become problematic.[33, p. 16] If it be granted that Libussa's love for man raises her above the selfishness of her sisters, then we may say that the tragedy lies in the fact that, as a gifted individual, she is repelled by many aspects of community life which she nevertheless regards as not only necessary but even desirable. For all the sombreness of her vision, she

insists that man is essentially good: once again Grillparzer
stresses that very little evil is due to outright villainy:

> Der Mensch ist gut, er hat nur viel zu schaffen,
> Und wie er einzeln dies und das besorgt,
> Entgeht ihm der Zusammenhang des Ganzen.
> Des Herzens Stimme schweigt, in dem Getöse
> Des lauten Tags unhörbar übertäubt.   (ll. 2461–5)

CHAPTER 5

GRILLPARZER'S CONCEPTION OF TRAGEDY

MANY tragedies contain the idea of a triumph over death. Such a feeling is given magnificent expression in the last speech of Milton's *Samson Agonistes*:

> Nothing is here for tears; nothing to wail
> Or knock the breast: no weakness nor contempt,
> Dispraise, or blame; nothing but well and fair,
> And what may quiet us in a death so noble.

Gilbert Murray notes that this idea that the spirit of man can conquer death is "the characteristic of Greek tragedy and the explanation of its undying influence". The Greeks of the fifth century B.C. were "ready to look straight at the most awful possibilities of life, to show men terrified by them, struggling with them, overthrown by them, so long as by some loftiness in the presentation or some nobility in the characters or perhaps some sheer beauty and inspiration in the poetry, one could feel in the end not defeat but victory, the victory of the spirit of man over the alien forces among which he has his being".*

When Grillparzer began his career, the German stage was dominated by Schiller's plays, which likewise do not depict unrelieved tragedy. Max Piccolomini, for instance, achieves moral greatness by choosing to die rather than betray his principles. His (and our) sadness is mitigated by the consciousness that he has

---

*Ref. 30, p. 8. On pp. 6–7 he gives the anthropological grounds why Greek tragedy came to embody the idea of a triumph over death.

acted rightly in appallingly difficult circumstances. It was Schiller's view that the pleasure we take in tragic misfortune depends on our perceiving that morally upright behaviour is still possible, even in the most difficult situations. This perception, he argued, makes us conscious that our own moral strength need never be impaired, which gives us an exhilarating feeling of our own power that is naturally pleasurable.

In Grillparzer's plays there is nothing of this kind to lessen the completeness of the tragedy. His heroes and heroines often do not achieve moral fulfilment, but come to grief because the rational and moral side of their natures is overwhelmed by emotions which grip them to the exclusion of all else. Medea and Hero are both convinced, initially, that they know themselves and are clear as to what it is they want from life. In *Der Gastfreund* Medea is completely self-willed and proclaims her independence from all ties (ll. 71–4). When her friend Peritta excuses a love-visit to a shepherd, saying:

> Es riß mich hin, ich war besinnungslos,
> Und nicht mit meinem Willen, nein—

Medea interrupts, and says scornfully:

> Ei hört!
> Sie wollte nicht, und tat's!—Geh! du sprichst Unsinn!
> Wie konnt' es denn geschehn,
> Wenn du nicht *wolltest*? Was ich tu', das will ich.

Hero too is initially full of confidence in herself, and says to her uncle "Laß mich so wie ich bin, ich bin es gern" (l. 138). In both plays the outcome is tragic because strong emotions are evoked in the heroines which annihilate this will-power. And they both express in very similar terms their bewilderment at their desertion of all they had formerly held dear. After she has twice saved Jason's life, Medea says:

> Es gibt ein Etwas in des Menschen Wesen,
> Das, unabhängig von des Eigners Willen,
> Anzieht und abstößt mit blinder Gewalt.
> (*Die Argonauten*, ll. 1012–14)

And Hero, when she finds herself trembling for Leander's safety, asks:

> Was ist es, das den Menschen so umnachtet
> Und ihn entfremdet sich, dem eignen Selbst,
> Und fremdem dienstbar macht?   (ll. 1177–9)

Grillparzer's Medea and Schiller's Johanna bring out the contrast between the two types of tragedy. Both heroines fall in love at first sight with the enemy they feel they ought to hate and kill; both are determined not to let this passion rule them, and for this reason both strive to avoid, at all cost, a further meeting with the man who has thus alienated them from what they regard as their true selves. But when the dreaded meeting takes place the two behave quite differently. Johanna, face to face with Lionel, decides to do her duty and thinks only of fulfilling her mission and freeing her country from the hated enemy. Medea, however, is paralysed, betrays her country, and can do nothing against Jason.

Ottokar's tragedy does not, at first sight, seem similar, for while Medea and Hero have their will-power undermined, his tragedy derives from his excess of will-power in the form of egoistic self-assertion. But in all three plays the sequence is really the same. We have, at the beginning, one who might well find happiness and fulfilment, but who is then placed in circumstances which stimulate strong emotions (in the case of Ottokar, ambition and the desire to possess more and more) which become so powerful that they silence all other tendencies in the character, and lead to destruction. This sequence is already clearly discernible in the early *Die Ahnfrau*, where Jaromir becomes a robber and murderer because he was kidnapped and brought up among thieves. Once again, the environment brings out the worst in a noble, high-minded young man.

Grillparzer has recorded that this, for him, was the essence of tragedy. He first stressed the powerful way in which human instincts can be stimulated by circumstances. Drama, he said, shows us (among other things) "das Notwendige", which includes "alles . . . was durch die unbezweifelte Einwirkung auf die untern, unwillkürlichen Triebfedern seiner [des Menschen] Handlungen, die Äußerungen seiner Thätigkeit, zwar nicht nötigend, aber doch anregend bestimmt". He continues:

> Die Einwirkung dieser äußern Triebfedern ist bekanntlich so stark, daß sie bei Menschen von heftigen (durch verkehrte Erziehung und unglückliches Temperament genährten) Neigungen oft alle Tätigkeit der Freiheit aufzuheben scheint, und selbst die Besten unter uns sind sich bewußt, wie oft sie dadurch zum Schlimmen fortgerissen wurden, und wie diese Triebfedern einen Grad von extensiver und intensiver Größe erreichen können, wo fast nur ein halbes Wunder möglich machen kann, ihnen zu entgehen.

Then he affirmed that this is precisely what the spectator of a tragedy ("der Mensch") witnesses: "Das Tragische . . . liegt darin, daß Mensch das Nichtige des Irdischen erkennt, die Gefahren sieht, welchen der Beste ausgesetzt ist und oft unterliegt" (I, 14, 31–2). Grillparzer's method of making the spectator perceive these things is to give the tragic hero himself a final awareness of them. This is why Grillparzer's fifth Acts are often felt to be something in the nature of epilogues in which the characters adopt new and unexpected attitudes after the tragic catastrophe. They come to realize how blind their behaviour had been so long as it was directed by an all-consuming passion. Thus Medea gives a final indictment of Jason's ruthless ambition and of her own passionate response to the way he had trampled upon her in trying to fulfil it. Ottokar, as he finally kneels to the dead Margarete, recognizes that his pride and ambition have blindly driven him to the death in battle which he knows awaits him. Mathias, at the end of *Ein Bruderzwist*, sees that his will to power has brought him not success, but a situation which he cannot control. And in Act V of *Die Jüdin* the king is likewise emptied of the passion that has hitherto directed him, and has come to repent it. There is nothing implausible in the final gentle contrition of all these characters, however unexpectedly it comes after their previous passionate behaviour. When their actions have brought not success but grief and catastrophe, morally upright men and women are naturally given pause. If Ottokar had been a hideous character from birth, it might be implausible to make him see the error of his ways in Act V. But in fact he might (as Rudolf tells him, ll. 1881–3) have become the best of men if his protracted good fortune had not fanned his least pleasant traits.

Many critics have supposed that the tragic outcome in Grillparzer's plays follows from the mere activity of the characters. Staiger[45, pp. 170, 182] writes of a "Fluch der Tat überhaupt" which compels Ottokar to commit evil since all action must necessarily be ruthless. But he has to concede that this is not so in the case of Ottokar's opponent Rudolf I: "Jede seiner Taten ist rein, weil sie im Namen des Ganzen und des Herrn des Ganzen, Gottes, geschieht." So there appears to be no "Fluch der Tat überhaupt" after all! Papst thinks the tragic outcome derives from the hero's failure to preserve "Sammlung" ("an intact state of collected composure") and from his surrender to *Tatendrang* which urged the self to seek apparent fulfilment through active participation in the tumult of life."[32, p. xii] He seems to suppose that, in Grillparzer's view, the contemplative life will be serene, the active one tragic. But this again is not substantiated by the career of Rudolf I, nor by that of Grillparzer's Rudolf II, whose tragedy derives from failure to take the right political action at the right moment (see above, p. 120). Some of his acts (e.g. towards Russworm and Cäsar) are pure and some of his contemplation (e.g. on alchemy) gives others their chance to undo him.

If it is alleged that tragedy results from loss of a certain psychological condition, then we must be able to form a clear idea of wherein this condition consists if we are to understand the derivation of the tragedy. But (in a later work) Papst defines "Sammlung" in such a way that it ceases to be an intelligible psychological state. "*Sammlung*", he says, "refers to a state of irreducible wholeness of being and recollected composure in which the self at once possesses, fulfils and transcends itself."[33, p. 12] Recent German critics have likewise invoked psychological mechanisms that I find unintelligible.*

In the portrayal of human behaviour there are three main possibilities. The dramatist can encourage us to identify ourselves with the hero, or the principal character can be presented as having all the faults and shortcomings which are (of course!) absent in ourselves, but which we recognize in our neighbours. The third possibility is when we neither identify ourselves with the hero nor dissociate ourselves from him, but say rather: there, but for the grace of God, go I: here is one, partly good, partly bad, like myself. Schiller chooses the first of these three possibilities; what his hero or heroine finally does we would do, or would wish to do, in similar circumstances. Wallenstein and Demetrius are exceptions, but the rule is well exemplified by Max Piccolomini, Maria and Johanna—idealists whose behaviour finally fills us with enthusiasm. Grillparzer, the realist, chooses the third possibility. The spectator of a tragedy "sieht die Gefahren, welchen der Beste ausgesetzt ist und oft unterliegt. . . . Er bedauert den strauchelnden Mitmenschen und hört nicht auf, den fallenden zu lieben"— because he recognizes how easily he too could fall.

If this third method of portrayal is fully effective, the hero never forfeits our sympathy entirely. Grillparzer deviated considerably from the details of the Medea legend and from the historical records concerning Ottokar and Rudolf II in order to make these characters more sympathetic. Sometimes he succeeds in eliciting our sympathy not only for the principal character, but also for those who work against him, so that we find their behaviour too both plausible and morally defensible. Thus we do not feel that he takes Hero's side against the priest, her uncle. Both enlist sympathy and understanding, and what each of them does not only

---

*Naumann affirms that Ottokar is a hero "der erst, durch seinen Untergang die Wahrheit des 'Substantiellen' (Hegel), das er durch seine Existenz geleugnet hatte, bestätigt".[31, p. 415] Partl specifies Grillparzer's method as "im Scheitern der Existenz die tragische Spannung zum Absoluten zu realisieren".[34, p. 253] The best discussion of Grillparzer's theory of tragedy and of its relation to his plays is still that of Strich,[49] to which I am deeply indebted.

seems inevitable, given their character and circumstances, but also devoid of malice or villainy (although, as we saw, Grillparzer felt that he had fallen short of this ideal in the case of the priest's behaviour in Act V). In *Ein treuer Diener* we sympathize with Simon and Peter when they work against Bancbanus, as well as with Bancbanus himself. But in this play the sequence of events is somewhat different from that in those to which I have been referring. Bancbanus is a tragic figure because of what he is in his particular situation, not because of what he becomes in it. Unlike Medea or Hero he is not swept by emotions which bewilder him. Unlike Ottokar he does not come to be ruled by egoism. All his thought and feeling is from first to last focused on one unselfish end. But it is his very selfless rectitude that brings disaster upon him. If he were more capable of anger or guile he would be more respected and feared.

In Grillparzer's tragedies, then, we see that a man's best talents and endowments are often smothered by his other tendencies or themselves lead directly to disaster. We in the twentieth century are used to the sheer unmitigated tragedy that has characterized European drama since Ibsen, but Grillparzer's pessimism came as something of an innovation—the beginning of the reaction against the underlying optimism of so much of eighteenth-century thought (a reaction expressed very forcibly by his contemporaries Schopenhauer and Leopardi).

But if tragedy teaches us the nullity of much that we seek, why do we take pleasure in it? Given Schiller's theory our pleasure is quite intelligible. His tragedies make us feel that the spirit of man is unconquerable: we see that the enemy can capture and enchain Johanna and behead Maria, but cannot prevent the spirit of either from rising to moral heights. And to see that such spiritual triumph is possible in adversity naturally gives pleasure. But how can we find it pleasurable to be shown the best of men losing their moral control? Grillparzer answers as follows, in a diary entry of 1820:

> Offenbar liegt ein Theil des Grundes von dem Wohlgefallen an dem Tragischen in der Poesie auch darin, daß der unbestimmte, formlose

Schmerz über die Übel des Lebens durch die bildende Kunst Gestalt
bekommt und nun nicht mehr als ein Unbegränztes in dumpfer Marter,
sondern als ein zu Überschauendes bei vollem Bewußtsein wirkt.
(II, 7, 291.)

Thus the vague sadness we often feel about man's misfortunes is
transmuted by tragedy into something much clearer; we are
brought to see that, man's nature being what it is, tragic experience is often inevitable for him; and our insight into how this can
and must come about makes us a spectator looking down, as it
were, on the human scene from a superior viewpoint. This
consciousness of our superior insight and understanding gives us
a feeling of power and strength which is essentially pleasurable.
While we understand, the human race we survey can only suffer
blindly, and to contemplate man's lot from such a standpoint can
be an exhilarating experience.

Grillparzer stated that the greater understanding of ourselves
and our neighbour that this experience brings may also make us
more tolerant, although in the same passage he insisted that true
art has no didactic aims. And he, of course, rejected any suggestion
that a play teaches us trite moral (or other) propositions. "Das
Theater ist kein Korrekzionshaus für Spitzbuben und keine
Trivialschule für Unmündige" (I, 14, 32). We are not meant to
learn from Phaon's rejection of Sappho in favour of Melitta that
"gleich und gleich gesellt sich gern", nor from Ottokar's career
that pride comes before a fall. Any cabby, he said, is capable of
ideas such as these,* and in *König Ottokar* it is the prosaic Mayor
of Prague who (in the presence of the humiliated king) is made to
voice the platitude: "Ja, Hochmut kommt zu Fall; ich sagt es
oft!" (l. 2050). The dramatist's purpose, as Grillparzer sees it, is
neither to instruct nor to give mere pleasure—that, he says, would
class the artist with the conjurer—but to exhilarate, to effect what
he specifies as:

die Erbehung des Geistes, die Erhöhung des ganzen Daseyns, das
Thätigwerden von Gefühlen, die oft im ganzen wirklichen Leben eines

---

*"Ideen . . . wie sie die Fiaker auch haben" (I, 1, lxxxiv n.).

Menschen nicht in Anregung kommen, den Überblick über das Ganze des Lebens, die Einsicht in die eigne Brust, in das Getrieb eigner und fremder Leidenschaften, das Wacherhalten des Enthusiasmus jeder Art, den die engen Verhältniße der Bürgerwelt so leicht einschläfern. (II, 7, 332.)

This passage—and also Grillparzer's comments on his own plays —make it clear that the reflections they stimulate are not meant to be restricted to the single theme of one human tendency coming to dominate others. He writes here of poetry affording "den Überblick über das Ganze des Lebens", and in *Das goldene Vließ*, for instance, he portrayed what he called the tragedy of life, showing how great expectations and achievements can lead ultimately to the conviction that nothing is worth achieving. Again, in *Ein Bruderzwist* Rudolf II has his judgement impaired by anger and resentment so that he eventually takes the political action from which he had hitherto wisely refrained. But the play presents much more than this further example of one tendency overriding others. Its portrayal of the situation culminating in the war of 1618 brings us to reflect how often a disaster has been initiated by short-sightedness and ignorance; how those who counsel restraint are thrust aside by enthusiasts oblivious of the danger, or have their own judgement finally warped by anger at the folly of their fellows. *Ein Bruderzwist* is one of Grillparzer's most effective plays because it compels us to so many reflections on life which we know to be true (although, as he was quite aware, they do not constitute a profound philosophy and lose most of their attraction when divorced from the concrete particulars of the play which suggests them).* This play thus forms the other extreme to *Die Ahnfrau* which can only achieve effectiveness by evoking the idea that life is controlled by a malignant fate—an idea which, as Grillparzer well knew (see above, p. 11) does not survive rational scrutiny. He found the position of the modern poet so difficult precisely because so much of what the older poets

*"Worin liegt es denn nun, daß das poetische Bild . . . einen Eindruck macht, den die zu Grunde liegende Wahrheit ewig nimmer machen würde? Darin, . . . daß ein wirklich existierendes Staubkörnchen mehr Überzeugung mit sich führt, als all die erhabenen Ideen, die unserer geistigen Bildung zu Grunde liegen sollen, oder wirklich liegen" (II, 10, 204).

suggest is now known to be false.* And only in this early tragedy and in his comedy *Weh dem, der lügt!* did he dare rely to any extent on the evocation of what he called "eigentlich absurde ... Vorstellungen".

As we should expect, Grillparzer believes that a work is usually more effective if it does not state its commentary on life, but compels the reader or audience to make it for themselves. Great poets, he says, "haben meistens den Gang der Natur zum Muster genommen, die Ideen anregt, aber vom lebendigen Faktum ausgeht" (I, 14, 83). The sight of a tree that has been struck by lightning may, he says, prompt sad reflections about "das Los des Schönen auf der Erde". These are not in the tree but are naturally elicited by its effect on the thoughtful and sensitive man. A painting, he adds, will concentrate on those features of a natural object that produce effects of this kind, and by his skilful selection of appropriate detail the artist will stimulate them even in less sensitive people who would not have been moved by the original:† the playwright should likewise evoke ideas in this indirect way:

> Freilich beruht die ganze Wirkung der Poesie darauf, daß der gewählte Fall auf viele ähnlicher Art Anwendung leidet—nur dadurch entsteht Teilnahme in der Brust des Lesers. Diese Generalisierung braucht aber

---

*"Beim Fortschritt der Kenntnisse ist das Gefühl für die Wahrscheinlichkeit zu einer Feinheit ausgebildet, von der man zu Zeiten Lope de Vegas keine Vorstellung hatte." German poetry in particular post-dates the rise of science and is therefore "lauter Sinn", not "eine Art Unsinn" as poetry should be (II, 10, 230). The context shows that he is complaining of poetry that is too intellectual. He cannot mean that poetry is properly gibberish or mysticism, for he repeatedly repudiates such a standpoint. Thus he says (again in a context criticizing the intellectual poetry of Germany): "Alle unsere Vorstellungen von Existenz sind nur vom Existierenden abgezogen, und wenn man das Letztere aus den Augen verliert, so gibt es nur Träume und keine Wesen. . . . Die Kunst aber soll eine, wenn auch höhere Welt mit Wesen seyn, ein erhöhtes Wachen mit glänzenden Gestalten; nicht ein Schlaf voll Träume" (II, 7, 314–15).

†II, 7, 341–3. Grillparzer, then, rejects the view that "art imitates nature". In a "Totengespräch" between Frederick the Great and Lessing he makes the former say: "Die Kunst beruht auf einer Steigerung des Wirklichen und unterscheidet sich eben dadurch von der Natur" (I, 13, 136).

> nur als dunkles Gefühl den Eindruck des Werkes zu begleiten, ohne sich lehrhaft und ausgesprochen als Satz und Beweis anzukündigen oder vorzudrängen (I, 15, 39).

In any case, he says, the poet is often not conscious of these underlying ideas. Grillparzer finds that the burden of *Hamlet* is "die Schwermut, in die der Mensch geräth, wenn er durch *gerechte* Bedenklichkeiten am Handeln gehindert wird". But he adds: "Nicht als ob Shakespeare das gedacht hätte, denn derlei Abstrakta fallen einem ächten Dichter beim Selbstschaffen nicht ein, es liegt aber zum Grunde" (II, 10, 323).

He reaches the conclusion that it is the function of drama to provide "ein Stück Leben" (II, 11, 202)—not a detailed copy of it, nor a mere portrayal of ideas, but a selection of those aspects and features of reality which will evoke ideas. He views all poetry in the same way:

> Allerdings muß jedem Gedicht, wie jedem menschichen Bestreben, eine Intenzion, ein Gedanke oder . . . eine Idee zum Grunde liegen. Andererseits aber soll das Gedicht ein Lebendiges sein und alles Lebendig-Wirkliche ist ein Konkretum, der Gedanke aber oder die Idee ist und bleibt ein Abstraktes . . . Glücklicherweise aber—um jene beiden Faktoren: Leben und Idee miteinander zu verknüpfen—findet sich, daß bei jedem vollkommenen Wirklichen, und wäre es nur ein Baum oder eine Landschaft, sich aus dem Beschauen heraus von selbst eine Idee dem Sinneseindruck zugesellt. . . . Der Kunstsinn ist eben die Gabe, den Gedanken im Bilde und nur im Bilde zu genießen. (I, 14, 110-12.)

From this standpoint features of Grillparzer's technique that we have repeatedly observed become intelligible; his preference, for instance, of direct action to narrative; his expression of ideas and emotions not by words alone, but by such visible means as gestures. In an instructive passage on the origin of language he discusses the difficulty of communicating emotions, and says it does not lie in finding signs with which to express them, but in ensuring that these signs are interpreted in the sense intended. The only signs that are self-explanatory, he adds, are gestures, and so "die erste Sprache wird daher eine Geberdensprache gewesen seyn. Diese ist dem Menschen so natürlich, daß wir noch jetzt unsere Wortsprache mit Geberden begleiten" (II, 11, 270).

From Grillparzer's viewpoint the development of German literature in the nineteenth century necessarily appeared as a decline. Poets were either recording the most trivial details of their environment, or else obsessed with grandiose ideas for which they could find no adequate visible or plastic expression. He saw around him on the one hand "die Dichter des Wirklich-Wahren, die nämlich ihre eigenen lumpigen Zustände für ... bedeutend hielten", and on the other "die Ideendichter, die irgend einem halbverrückten Satze einen ganz ausgerenkten und verkrüppelten Körper anzupassen strebten" (I, 14, 166). This was written in the 1860's and had he survived into the 1890's he would have had more to say in criticism of poets of the former kind. But most of his scorn is in fact directed against the latter group, since the Germany of his experience was dominated by transcendental philosophy, particularly by Hegel whose work he designated "die monströseste Ausgeburt des menschlichen Eigendünkels" (II, 12, 40). In a typical passage he cries:

> Nun kommen aber unsere neueren poetischen Stümper und raffen von allen Seiten Riesenideen zusammen, die wie natürlich, ihnen nicht gehören, indes was ihnen gehört: Darstellung, Formgebung, Belebung, so erbärmlich ist, daß man damit nicht eine Maus beleben könnte. (I, 14, 111.)

He considered that it was Austria's good fortune to have been spared the ill-effects which progress in science and speculation in philosophy had had on German literature. Much has recently been written on the specifically Austrian characteristics of Grillparzer's writing.* He himself found it characteristic of the Austrian literature of his day that it had managed to preserve what German art had lost, namely "ein warmes Herz, einen offenen Sinn und Natürlichkeit" (I, 14, 153).

---

*See, for instance, Baumann.[5]

NUMBERED LIST OF REFERENCES

Abbreviations.

DD = *Das deutsche Drama vom Barock bis zur Gegenwart. Interpretationen,* hrsg. B. von Wiese, Bagel, Düsseldorf, 1958, Bd. I.

G = Grillparzer.

GLL = *German Life and Letters, New Series,* Blackwell, Oxford.

JGG = *Jahrbuch der Grillparzergesellschaft,* Konegen, etc., Wien.

MLR = *Modern Language Review,* publ. by Modern Humanities Research Association.

The following list is not intended as a bibliography of the secondary literature on G. Adequate bibliographies have already been printed and are listed on p. x above.

1. ATKINSON, M. E., G's use of symbol and image in "Des Meeres und der Liebe Wellen", *GLL*, IV, 1951.
2. ATKINSON, M. E. edn. of Tieck, *Der Blonde Eckbert,* Blackwell, Oxford, 1952.
3. BACKMANN, R., Vom Werdegang des "Goldenen Vließes," *G-studien,* ed. Kataan, Gerlach & Wiedling, Wien, 1924.
4. BAUMANN, G., "*Ein Bruderzwist in Habsburg*", *DD.*
5. BAUMANN, G., *G. Dichtung und österreichische Geistesverfassung,* Athenäum Verlag, Frankfurt, 1966.
6. BLACKALL, E. A., "Die Jüdin von Toledo", *German Studies presented to W. Bruford,* Harrap, London, 1962.
7. CARLYLE, T., German playwrights, *Critical and Miscellaneous Essays,* Chapman & Hall, London, 1894, vol. I.
8. COENAN, F. E., *G's Portraiture of Men, Univ. of N. Carolina Studies in the Germanic Langs. and Lits.,* No. 4, Chapel Hill, 1951.
9. CRAIG HOUSTON, G., *The Evolution of the Historical Drama in Germany during the First Half of the Nineteenth Century,* Mullan, Belfast, 1920.
10. CURME, G. O., edn. of G's *Libussa,* Frowde, New York, 1913.
11. EHRHARD, A., *G : le théâtre en Autriche,* Société d'Imprimerie, Paris, 1900.
12. EMRICH, B., art. Biedermeier, *Reallexikon der Deutschen Literaturgesch.,* 2 Aufl., hrsg. W. Kohlschmidt, de Gruyter, Berlin, 1958.
13. FARINELLI, A., *G und Lope de Vega,* Felber, Berlin, 1894.
14. FOGLAR, A., *Gs Ansichten über Literatur. Bühne und Leben,* 2 Aufl., Göschen, Stuttgart, 1891.
15. FUERST, N., *G auf der Bühne,* Mantius, Wien, 1958.
16. GARDINER, S. R., *The Thirty Years' War,* Longmans Green, London, 1874.

17. HEBBEL, F., "Die Ahnfrau" von G, *Werke, hist.-krit. Ausgabe*, ed. WERNER, Behr, Berlin, 1903, Bd. XI.
18. HOCK, E., "Libussa", *DD*.
19. HOCK, S., *Gs Werke*, Tl. IV, Bong, Berlin, etc., n.d.
20. HUBER, W., G als religiöser Denker, *JGG*. XXXIV, 1937.
21. KATAAN, O., "Weh dem, der lügt!" und das Problem der Wahrhaftigkeit, *G-studien* (as under (3) above).
22. KLAAR, A., *"König Ottokar" : Eine Untersuchung über die Quellen*, Freytag, Leipzig, 1885.
23. KOHM, J., *"Die Ahnfrau" in ihrer gegenwärtigen und früheren Gestalt*, Konegen, Wien, 1903.
24. KRISPYN, E., G's tragedy "Die Jüdin von Toledo", *MLR*, LX, 1965.
25. LESSING, O. E., Schillers Einfluß auf G, *Bulletin of Univ. of Wisconsin, Philos. and Lit. Series*, LIV, 1902.
26. LESSING, O. E., *G und das Neue Drama*, Piper, Leipzig, 1905.
27. MINOR, J., *Zur Gesch. der deutschen Schicksalstragödie und zur Gs* "Ahnfrau", *JGG*, IX, 1899.
28. MINOR, J., Das Schicksalsdrama, in KÜRSCHNER, *Deutche National Literatur*, CLI.
29. MORRIS, I. V., The "Ahnfrau" controversy, *MLR*, LXII, 1967.
30. MURRAY, G., *Aeschylus*, Clarendon Press, Oxford, 1940.
31. NAUMANN, W., "König Ottokar", *DD*.
32. PAPST, E. E., edn. of *Der arme Spielmann*, Nelson, London, 1960.
33. PAPST, E. E., G's "Des Meeres und der Liebe Wellen", *Studies in German Lit.*, ed. FORSTER and ROWLEY, No. 9, Arnold, London, 1967.
34. PARTL, K., Schillers "Wallenstein" und Gs "König Ottokar", *Abhandlungen zur Kunst-. Musik-. und Literaturwissenschaft*, Bonn, 1960, VIII.
35. PAULSEN, W., *"Die Ahnfrau" : zu Gs früher Dramatik*, Niemeyer, Tübingen, 1962.
36. RANKE, L. VON, *Vom Religionsfrieden bis zum dreißigjährigen Kriege*, in *Sämtliche Werke*, 54-vol. edn., Duncker & Humblot, Leipzig, 1868, VII.
37. REDLICH, O., *Gs Verhältnis zur Geschichte*, Gerold, Wien, 1901.
38. RIPPMANN, W., edn. of *Sappho*, MacMillan, London, 1942.
39. RITTER, M., *Deutsche Geschichte im Zeitalter der Gegenreformation*, Cotta, Stuttgart, 1895, II.
40. ROMMEL, O., *Die alt-wiener Volkskomödie. Ihre Geschichte vom barocken Welttheater bis zum Tode Nestroys*, Schroll, Wien, 1952.
41. SAUER, A., Ein treuer Diener seines Herrn, *JGG*, III, 1893.
42. SCHERER, W., G, in *Vorträge und Aufsätze zur Gesch. des geistigen Lebens in Deutschland und Österreich*, Weidmann, Berlin, 1874.
43. SENGLE, F., *Das deutche Geschichtsdrama*, Metzler, Stuttgart, 1952.
44. STAHL, E. L., Das Schauspiel der Schillerepigonen, *Theatergeschichtliche Forschungen*, XXI, 1910.
45. STAIGER, E., "König Ottokar", *Meisterwerke deutscher Sprache aus dem neunzehnten Jarhundert*, 3. Aufl., Atlantis, Zürich, 1957.
46. STEIN, G., *The inspiration motif in the works of G*, Nijhoff, The Hague, 1955.

47. STIEFEL, R., Gs "Goldenes Vließ", *Basler Studien zur deutschen Sprache und Literatur*, Hft. 21, 1959.
48. STIEVE, F., art. Rudolf II, *Allgemeine deutsche Biographie*, Bd. XXIX, Duncker & Humblot, Leipzig, 1889.
49. STRICH, F., Gs Aesthetik, *Forschungen zur neueren Literaturgeschichte*, XXIX, 1905.
50. TIECK, L., Schillers "Wallenstein", *Kritische Schriften*, Brockhaus, Leipzig, 1852, Bd. III.
51. WATERHOUSE, G., edn. of *Weh dem, der Lügt!*, 4th edn., Manchester Univ. Press, 1962.
52. WELLS, G. A., The problem of right conduct in "Ein Bruderzwist", *GLL*, XI, 1958.
53. WELLS, G. A., Fate-tragedy and "Die Braut von Messina", *Journal of English and Germanic Philology*, LXIV, 1965.
54. WURZBACH, W. VON, Die Jüdin von Toledo in Geschichte und Dichtung, *JGG*, IX, 1899.
55. YATES, D., *G : a Critical Biography*, Blackwell, Oxford, 1946 (repr. 1964).
56. YUILL, W. E., edn. of *Der Traum ein Leben*, Nelson, London, 1955.

INDEX OF AUTHORS

INDEX OF PLAYS

173